Let's
Light
One Up

Karl Albert May

1st Edition

Table of Contents

Dedication Page

First of all, I dedicate this book to my family and to my wife and daughter, because without them my life would be truly incomplete.

Also, to all of the husbands, wives, mothers, fathers, children, brothers, sisters, aunts, uncles, cousins, friends and anyone else who maybe suffering as the result of an addiction. I share in your pain and understand the sense of helplessness that's associated with it.

Lastly to the addicts who will possibly suffer great loss, or perhaps even die today. Often these losses can occur for no other reason than the lack of proper methods to help them overcome their addiction.

Preface

I realize there could be some false interpretations with the title of my book, especially for those hoping the invitation was going to be literal! Instead though it's completely metaphorical, representing a figurative light illuminating what I believe to be a slightly different road to overcoming addictions. During the process of writing this book, I debated several times whether or not to change the title to "The Fictitiousness of Addictiveness". Honestly I found it to be kind of catchy to say, but really I considered changing it for the simple fact that there are so many misconceptions surrounding the subject of Addiction and Recovery (now abbreviated as A&R). Mostly they've originated from excuses commonly used by addicts, explaining why they have such a lack of self-control. You know the ones I'm talking about like, "I just can't stop the monster inside of me", or "once you're an addict you're always an addict". However, you can't solely hold them responsible for making up those excuses all on their own, as many of them were fabricated from ideas they've picked up from the various A&R programs out there. Let's not forget to mention as well, the erroneous advice given by those who've never truly been addicted, but yet are deemed as experts for their "achievements" in interpreting human behavior. They've contributed to the confusion by introducing many inaccurate diagnoses of the psychological imbalances of the addict. The one that I'm personally most disturbed about is the one suggesting that addiction is somehow a disease or disorder. Whether this idea can be proven or not, this is so detrimental to the addicts recovery, because it simply adds more excuses to their already enormous list of reasons as to why they're unable to control themselves in the first place.

It's due to the existence of these types of misconceptions and the general confusion surrounding the subject of A&R, I was compelled to seek out my own alternate solutions to overcoming addictions. During my research, I've uncovered quite a few misinterpretations even within the definition of the word itself. One such inaccuracy defines addiction as an "uncontrollable compulsion", suggesting that an addict is incapable of control. However, this is easily proven false, as anyone who's successfully overcome an addiction would've needed to exhibit some level of control in order to do so. How then would I define addiction? I'd say it's an illogical series of decisions to compulsively abuse a substance, or to indulge in a physical act for the purposes of generating pleasure, or altering reality. These often detrimental decisions are typically followed by a perpetuating abandonment of self control, which if unchanged, is fully capable of leaving the addict in a state of absolute despair or worse.

So I hope to explain how I've discovered a slightly different way to overcome addictions. I contribute this accomplishment to my comprehension and application of certain "wisdoms", which unfortunately, I didn't find spelled out in just one particular place. This discovery required much reading, self-evaluation, revelation and not to mention twenty-five years of repeatedly falling on my face in order to discover. I've also learned the hard way, through personal experience, that the consequences of not overcoming addiction has more than sufficient potential to destroy a person! That may seem a bit overdramatic to some, particularly those who believe that only the more serious types of addictions would be capable of destroying someone. You know, addictions to the hard-core drugs, such as heroine, cocaine, crystal meth and the like. I'd have to completely disagree as my addictions were not to those types of drugs, yet all but left my life in a state of total ruin! It's therefore my full conviction that addictions of any nature, including the ones which seem "harmless", are still very capable of destroying our lives.

What I also hope to do, is fully acquaint you with the ideas that brought me into the freedom I now enjoy. What's great about what I've learned, is you won't have to search in some far off distant land for the answers to overcoming your addictions. It won't be necessary to "pray" to receive anything, as this ability isn't reserved for some chosen few. There won't be any prescription drugs or patches that you'll need to replace your addictions with either. Truly what I've discovered is available to anyone willing to learn about it, and who will simply apply it to their life. If you don't believe such an ability exists, you're perfectly capable of ignoring it and just remain how you are now. I can't imagine though why anyone would purposely choose not to learn more, especially if they came to realize the potential of this ability.

Just so you're aware, even though I did indeed set out to write a book to hopefully influence a significant number of peoples lives, I didn't write it as an end all of books on A&R. Rather I hoped it would be a tool in the belt of someone wanting to truly improve themselves. I'd count it a blessing if it helps just one person to change the direction of their life and if it helps more than that, I'll count it as nothing short of extraordinary! I also don't claim the rights to the wisdoms I've revealed in this book. I didn't "corner the market"on the truth, I just wanted to put it in a slightly different way to perhaps make it a little easier for an addict who's wanting help with their life. Sincerely, I hope the answers you've been asking or praying for you'll find contained within the pages of this book. Regardless of how you receive those answers, it's my simple prayer you just do! For what it's worth, I earnestly poured all of my passion and thought into writing this, as I simply felt the need to share with the world the story of how I came to discover this amazing and powerful internal "ability".

Introduction

At this moment as you're reading these words, the after effects of addiction are ceaselessly ruining many peoples lives. Relationships and marriages are being destroyed, children and spouses are being physically beaten and abused and in many cases killed, as repercussion of the abuses of narcotics and behavioral addiction. Careers and businesses people have worked their whole lives to build, are being needlessly thrown away. As a society in general, our hope for a brighter tomorrow seems to be heavily shadowed by the selfishness that's overcome so many of us. Everyone is loosing on some level, addict or otherwise, to peoples dependencies to drugs, alcohol, sex, pornography, gambling and whatever other vices you can think of. It's not just the criminals and street thugs who are loosing either, it's hitting home and affecting all of us. This is mainly due to the fact that once a vice has begun to dominate the will of a person, it has the potential to take us straight to the bottom and unfortunately no one is exempt from that possibility. I believe it's past time for each member of our society to take some sort of action, as we're all affected by addiction in some way. I find the most effective way to do that, is to insure there are proper educational materials readily available to anyone willing to read them.

I must ask, are you reading this book because you're wanting answers and solutions to overcoming your own addictions? It's perfectly fine if you are, I promise you're not alone. In fact, it's probably safe to say that millions of other people around the world are searching for the exact same answers. This is the reason I decided to quit my business and means of livelihood in order to write it! I did it for the people who are truly wanting to change the direction of their life and who want to improve themselves. It's also for those who've had little to no success using traditional recovery programs, or who've taken the advice of medical professionals and Ph.D's and found themselves back in the same old place or worse. The solutions I offer are based upon what's worked for me and I sincerely believe they'll work for anyone who's willing to have an "open" mind.

Do me a favor before we begin and just try and imagine what your life would be like if you weren't in bondage to a drug or destructive behavioral pattern? A life in which your friendships and relationships are based around openness and honesty, instead of secrecy and deceitfulness? Where you posses the ability to control your actions and determine your path in life. Not only am I absolutely positive you can be freed from your addictions, but once you're free, you'll have a renewed self confidence like never before! This could easily excel your career, your relationships and help you advance in whatever area you want it to. However, you shouldn't wait to seek freedom from your addictions until after it's too late the way I did! You should seek to free yourself now. Anyway, you'll learn rather quickly when you're not being weighed down by a weakness in your character, you'll begin to build other strengths as well. After all, wouldn't you rather be a person of self-control than someone who grovels in the miserable darkness of selfishness?

Before you get too far along in my book, I must point out that I'm not formally educated in addictions counseling, nor am I certified to teach any traditional recovery programs. My level of education is measured by the experiences I've had as an addict and the lessons life has taught me thus far. My greatest achievement would be my discovery of the wisdom which has made it possible for me to overcome my addictions.

   If there are any of you reading this who happen to be addicted to what I refer to as the "hard-core drugs" like I've mentioned, such as heroine, cocaine, meth, etc, I would highly recommend going through the process of detoxification before you attempt to go any further unless you haven't used these drugs in a while. That being said, if you feel you're being "led" to read this anyway, please continue.

   In closing, I'm quite confident you'll be able to overcome any addiction you currently have, at least if you're able to comprehend and apply what I am about to reveal to you. You've already taken a huge step simply by choosing to read a book like this in the first place. However, don't be naïve either to the obstacles which are able to prevent you from discovering you're freedom. I've identified three basic character flaws you may want to work on if they apply to you, it's probably safe to say there's a good chance they probably do. They are, selfishness, ignorance and pride and they are the main causes of failure particularly during the process of recovery. Selfishness, because that's simply what addiction boils down to. Ignorance, because without proper wisdom you can't fully grasp the solutions to your problems. Lastly there's the subject of PRIDE, which in itself could be your downfall if your not careful. Especially if you're in denial that someone else besides yourself, may actually possess solutions and answers to overcoming your problems.

Chapter 1

Chapter 1 *A society of addicted people*

I wanted to discuss this topic in order to hopefully make you aware of just how common addiction is. If you will, try and grasp the wide scope of addictions which exist. Start with the ones you're familiar with, it shouldn't take long to discover that an entire book could be filled describing the many variances of them. I nearly added some statistics here to prove just how wide spread they are, but I'd likely be grossly underestimating the actual numbers of people addicted. Millions upon millions, would be a very conservative number. Make no mistake about it, it's easy to imagine just how true it is, that our world is indeed literally filled with addicts!

The common addictions

If you're taking the time to read this book, I assume at some point in your life you've suffered through an addiction, or perhaps you've known someone who has? It's due to this overwhelming realization of the magnitude of addiction, that I believe this

subject should be of interest to everyone.
I find the most commonly "recognized"
addictions are smoking and the abuse of
alcohol. Then there's the expanding
population of people who prefer the abuse
of the hard-core drugs and the multitudes
hooked on prescription drugs. However, I
believe the one addiction which is
capturing the most number of new "victims",
would be the sex industry. It's fueled by
prostitution, adult entertainment and last
but not least, the most, popular one of all
pornography. It also happens to be the
easiest and least obtrusive way to
participate in this industry, even more so
since the introduction of the world wide
web. This industry is largely to blame for
the increased criminal restlessness in our
society and the sexually abusive activities
plaguing the lives of men, woman and
children. There's also quite an increased
susceptibility of our youth to become
addicted to sex, due to the overwhelming
availability of sexually related material.
It's because of all of these facts, that
I'd seriously doubt anyone born in our
society, would be automatically immune to
the lure of addictive material. Therefore I
believe we should all be mindful that
addictive material is available at almost

every turn and has the power to capture our interest if we aren't aware of it. Any addiction can easily gain control over our "will", regardless of our stature or status, as there's no prejudice or preference to the type of individual who can be overcome.

Education is key.

I believe that it's of vital importance for the growth and mental stability of an individual to learn, even at a very early age, about addiction. If we don't warn our young people about the influences of addictive material or about this subject in general, they'll end up learning about it on their own through personal experience. In light of this, wouldn't you agree it's past time for the "hush-hush let's not talk about that" era to be over, especially since we're entering a whole new one anyway? Which era is that you ask? The one that's "rocking" our whole world right now. Only those who embrace the potentials of the human mind and eradicate the ignorances of the by-gone era, will be able to truly survive. So then, if you want to prepare yourself or others to handle the challenges of the the new world we're living in, we must do away with useless and ineffective educational materials. They need to be replaced with the improved ideas of our age, as they'll never fail to fuel progress at least if they're centered around truth and wisdom. However, there are a lot of primitive materials available (especially to addicts) which unfortunately do little more than promote mental slavery. Bottom line is that we're doomed to failure if continue to buy into lies suggesting someone else will create change for us from "something" outside of ourselves.

It's not too late to turn it around

There are ways of reversing the degradation of our culture and eradicating the ignorances preventing us from advancing as a whole. It begins by focusing on solutions rather than enlarging problems, because which ever one receives the majority of our focus, will be the one to prevail. Anyway, I don't believe I'm alone in seeing the need to improve myself. I believe that in one way or another, we all desire to be liberated from vices prohibiting us from maintaining control of ourselves. After all the number one thing destroying our culture (and really any culture) is <u>selfishness.</u> I'm convinced it will not fail to finish it's work either, unless something is radically done to change it's current course. What work is that? That once selfishness has had an opportunity to run it's course in our lives, the only thing left behind is <u>self</u>. A life which is filled with self, is void of true love, friendship, and companionship and no one can thrive for long in this state. On the other hand, a life void of selfishness is filled with possibility, reward and hope.

In some way we're all called to make changes and improvements to ourselves wherever necessary and these changes aren't purely for the improvement of our own individual lives, but ultimately contributes to the good of all humanity. So then why procrastinate to make changes to your own life? Decide right now the type of role you will take in the advancement of our species.

Chapter 2

Chapter 2   *Are you an addict?*

I often find myself reiterating the meaning of the words addict and addiction, as they're commonly misunderstood. Lack of self-control is the cause of all irrational compulsive decisions, and these decisions aren't merely limited to hard-core addicts either. They're able to "control" anyone choosing to make similar types of decisions, particularly those unaware of any issues they might have. Most of these types of people are under a delusion that their compulsion or issue isn't really that big of a deal, when in reality, it maybe a full blown addiction. For those of you who already recognize the fact that you're an addict, I must congratulate you, as you're already halfway through your recovery! As for the other readers who have a compulsion or issue you don't recognize as an addiction, I ask only that you get real with yourself and be open to admitting that maybe something's controlling you and holding you back. It's likely the big white elephant you're trying to ignore right now and also the "thing" in the past that you've deemed as harmless. Maybe you're having a tough time admitting you have a problem, because it's often considered "socially unacceptable" to be categorized as an addict. Honestly it's ridiculous that there's such a stigma surrounding the subject of addiction in the first place, and it truly makes the available help virtually unusable. Especially to someone who might be sensitive to being labeled as an addict, or who doesn't feel comfortable in a group setting airing out their "dirt laundry".

I was a such a person, because I refused to accept that my addictions were "that big of a deal". If your thinking that way too, I'm here to get a little in your face and ruffle your collar a bit, and hopefully shake some sense into you. It's my conviction that if you're involved in "anything" you can't stop doing right at this very moment, you're indeed an addict and need help. Don't give me any lame excuses either, such as that you do it, simply because you enjoy it. Truth is, it's probably controlling you whether you realize it or not.

DUI, is it worth it?

This is the point in which the subject of addiction can get quite serious. It instantly becomes an entirely different issue if your addicted to something considered illegal, or if you're committing crimes as a result of being an addict. This whole subject actually makes me sick to my stomach when I really think about it, because at one time I was the derelict who frequently put himself and those around him at serious risk due to my poor decisions. All I have to say, is if you get behind the wheel of a car while under the influence of drugs or alcohol and feel alright about making that decision, you're most definitely a criminal and deserve to be in jail. There are no rational or sane people who truly care about themselves or others that would make a decision to put someone in harms way just to avoid having to pay for a cab or saving face. You say you can't afford a cab? Can you afford then to pay the penalty for killing someone, or potentially multiple someones over the cost of a cab fair? You know as well as the next guy, that driving under the influence kills people every single day. At least one every 39 minutes in fact. What's senseless is most of those deaths happen as a result of ignorant thinking, such as that they

drive better after they've been drinking.
I'm grateful I never killed anyone doing
the idiotic things I did, but now it's my
firm conviction that driving while under
the influence should carry the same
sentence as attempted murder. The hard
facts are, that getting behind the wheel of
a vehicle while intoxicated, is equivalent
to loading a pistol and waiving it around
intending to randomly killing someone.

I don't want to neglect to mention the
devastation caused by those abusing the
hard-core drugs either. Particularly the
ones capable of obliterating the minds
ability to reason. Not that there's a mind
altering chemical or substance which is
incapable of destroying someone, but there
are those particular drugs which cause
people to make even more drastic decisions
in their abuse of them. I'm talking about
the ones which are able to greatly inhibit
the logical processes of the brain.
Processes which would normally protect us
from doing harm to ourselves, but instead
become extremely illogical, causing any
number of life threatening scenarios. It's
usually the cravings produced by the
absence of these drugs in the body which
creates the more illogical decisions. The
primary motive of a mind that's left

craving these drugs, shifts only to re-creating the euphoric state once produced by them, regardless of the potential casualty or cost. It's while in this illogical state, that an addict will commit any number of crimes including, murder, theft (even from of a family member or friend) and quite often end up prostituting themselves just to get more money or drugs. I've heard of cases where addicts go so far as to even prostitute their children simply to feed their out of control addiction. What a tragic place for a anyone to be in! Despite these examples of heavy drug abuse, the fact still remains that any addiction can create a "mental dependency" and cause irrational decisions to be made and repeated.

I lost it all.

A few years ago I found out the hard way that this fact is quite true, as my entire life changed dramatically as a consequence of my multiple addictions. It began one afternoon after a phone call I received while I was at work. It was from my wife informing me that she'd packed up all her stuff and moved to her moms house.

She said that neither she, nor our daughter, would be home that afternoon when I got there. As soon as I got off the phone I immediately left work and drove home to discover not only had she packed all her belongings, she had taken all of my daughters furniture, clothes and decorations out of her room and truly had abandoned our home. She made it perfectly clear to me in a later phone conversation, that her intentions were to never return. I was to say the least, quite devastated. At that time we'd been married for 10+ years and had just one child together. Anyway, little did I know prior to her moving out, she'd already legally filled to divorce me as well. I was served divorce papers by a police officer the following weekend. That story could fill up an entire book on it's own, but what's important about that time, is that it eventually brought me into one serious "state of humility". Now after discovering the wisdom I have, I'm able to admit that one way or the other, my losses were due to the hold my addictions had on me. I'm wondering if you have anything to loose if your addiction isn't brought under control? Just so you know, my wife and I decided on our divorce date a year after she left to rectify our marriage and now we're back living together as a family!

I wasn't a "crack head".

I was never addicted to any of those "hard-core" drugs as I've already mentioned and the only recreational drug I ever tried was marijuana, but never overly enjoyed it that much to pursue it as a permanent way to get high. I did however discover how much I enjoyed the side effects of abusing the prescription drug Hydrocodone, (which is another form of the potent pain killer Codeine). I had actually became quite addicted to it and abused it until the doctor wouldn't write another prescription. So I eventually ran out and ended up replacing the addiction with something else. Some of things I became addicted to were potentially lethal, however the type of drugs you can be addicted to or the different behaviors you can exhibit, are completely irrelevant. What matters is that they can rob you of the things you care about, whether you think they can or not.

There's this comparison I'd like to make between the consequences of an addiction and the consequences of breaking the law. Rarely does it matter the nature of a crime, the reality is, if you're found guilty of committing one you could end up spending time in prison as punishment. How about an accountant who's been formally charged with committing tax fraud and has been sentenced to serve time in prison? Should they be considered anything less than a criminal because of the nature of their crime? That because he didn't rape or murder his victims, the way the guy in the cell next to him did, that he should somehow be able to avoid being labeled as a criminal? What if the things this accountant did financially destroyed someones life and the devastation caused their client to go crazy and commit suicide, are they morally any less of a murderer? This same applies to the addict, it doesn't matter if their drug of choice is to crack cocaine (which is a processed drug), or to dopamine (which is a natural drug released in the brain during sex or even when pornography is viewed), the consequences of either addiction can create equally devastating situations.

Addicts can easily become murderers.

Alcoholism has been considered by some to be an individual affliction. However behind the wheel of a car, an alcoholic can cause just as much harm as a terrorist with a bomb strapped to his chest. This also applies to the porn addict who sits at home or work all day and views pornography. Maybe he becomes bored with it and decides to move on to something more interactive, such as "chatting" with under age children about sex? If you've ever watched 20/20, you know this isn't a crime which is taken likely. The reality is that this person is quite capable of committing heinous crimes such as pursuing sex with an underage age child or worse. (just to clear the air, I never had any interest in chatting with anyone, much less a underage child). How about someone whose hooked on gambling and piss away their entire paycheck on Black Jack, are they any less susceptible to the consequences of financial destruction then the junkie whose addicted to crystal meth? The point I'm trying to make once again, is that the drug of choice is irrelevant, the type of addiction truly doesn't matter. What matters is that you can become a slave to any vice and therefore potentially harm yourself or other people. So hopefully

I've made it clear that any substance or
behavioral addiction that's left
uncontrolled, can lead to permanent loss of
life or liberty. Therefore if you're an
addict and can fully admit you're one and
are able to realize you may need help,
truly I'm able to sympathize with you. I'm
also here to confirm with absolute
certainty, that there's a way for you to
change the direction of your life. First
though, it's vitally important to come to
grips with the hold your addiction has on
you.

What's got you?

     This is the point when you need to
begin the process of examining yourself to
discover if there maybe an addiction
holding you back. It could be quite obvious
you're giving control over to something and
further examination is unnecessary. Just
in case though you can't quite put a finger
on an issue you may have, I'll provide a
few commonly overlooked addictions for you
to make a comparison with. First I'll
discuss the common addiction developed
while excessively playing video games and
participating in online gaming. I'm not

suggesting that playing video games is somehow immoral or wrong, so ease off with that accusation, if that's indeed what you're thinking. With that said, let's discuss what could be lurking behind this seemingly innocent pastime. I'll admit right off the bat, compared to someone who's married with kid's, a single person likely has much more free time to play video games. Regardless though of your marital status, you should still ask yourself if excessively playing video games is really helping you to become the best possible version of yourself? Couldn't you be making better use of your time? I think the answer is clear if you're being honest. The exception to this would be if you're planning on making a living as a video game evaluator, or as a professional gambler, then it would be quite acceptable. I'm however going to say, you're probably not going to benefit from hours upon hours of back to back video gaming. A little time spent in play is alright and probably healthy, but a lot of time spent in play is folly. There's no doubt in my mind that if you're excessively spending your time in any activity, you'll eventually reap the effects that such pursuits can have on your life.

Marriage, Kids and Video Games

    This sub-chapter is geared more toward the married couple. So if you're single you may want to skim over it. Anyway, the effects of excessive video game play are often far more evident in the married person, as you're clearly wasting time which could be spent with your spouse. I already hear the guys making up excuses such as, "she's always busy doing her own thing", or she's cutting coupons and doing housework, I don't want to bother her". I have to tell you straight up, that those are lame excuses! Here's a novel idea, how about helping her to do some housework or participating in what she's doing, so you're able to have some time to relate with each other! Balance and self-control is necessary in all of life and in this case spending quality time with your spouse will insure a happier marriage. Just by the slim chance you're thinking that you're addiction to playing video games won't destroy your marriage, I have some really bad news for you. It can and will, especially if you're spending more time touching your keyboard and mouse than your wife! I don't want to hear about how "strong willed" you are and how you can "keep it under control". That's just something all addicts say right before they're hooked! If you must play the games, play them together! I'd consider that acceptable and not a debilitating addiction (unless of course you both play all the time). If however you have kid's and you're playing a lot of video games while your kid's are at home or awake, I have to say that's a potential problem. Yes it's true your kids need time to play on their own and you need time to yourself, that's not the issue. You should be interacting with them and encouraging them to be active and to participate in activities as a family. I just so happen to know there are those of you who actually get mad at your kids for interrupting your "game time", even if you won't openly admit to it. Shouldn't you instead be teaching your children to be self-controlled rather than self-centered?

So, if you've compare your "insignificant issue" with those examples and you're still wondering whether or not you're an addict. Simply consider the fact that anything demanding large portions of your time, could be considered a lack of

self control and therefore an addiction.
Even a job where you aren't required to
work as long as you do, can end up being
one.

Lack of self-control?

Let's switch gears and discuss the age
old addiction of smoking cigarettes and how
it perfectly illustrates a lack of self-
control on the part of an addict. There are
probably some of you who'd disagree with
that statement and that's ok. Let me see
though if I can change your mind? Everyone
knows that smoking has been medically
proven to physically cause serious health
problems, they even put these warnings on
the packs now days. One of the issue is
that it greatly reduces the oxygen that
your lungs are able to process in order for
you to perform even the most simple of
tasks. It makes a 25 year old look like a
40 year old and it creates severe halitosis
(bad breath), which is extremely offensive
and not to mention, turns your teeth a
nasty chicken poop yellow brownish color.
Last but not least, it's the leading cause
of multiple types of cancer. You probably
already knew most those facts anyway

though, right? So, if you indeed acknowledging these facts and yet still continue to smoke, would you say those are decisions made by a person who's in control, or out of control? O.k, if you're still in denial that smoking is evidence of a weak and dependent character, let me dig a little more. I apologize if I'm making anyone uncomfortable here, but if you think this pressure is uncomfortable, how are you going to handle when your doctor informs you that cancer has spread throughout your body and you're going to be dead in a few months? Imagine telling your loved ones that due to your selfish decisions, they're going to have to suffer as result of what you chose to do to yourself. Maybe you don't care, or perhaps you're one of those types of people who don't believe something like that can happen to you? Anyway, if for any reason it's still a preposterous idea to admit that smoking's a weakness of character, I'll go ahead and bet ten to one you also buy into the philosophy that "life just happens"! Am I right? This philosophy is nothing short of pure ignorance, because it's totally up to you to decide how you're going to choose to live your life. Overcoming this feeble mindset, is where those of strong character are set-apart from the weak minded. Not to mention, where the rich and successful are often seperated from the failures and the poor. Really it's where any variance in character imaginable is found. People who succeed, purposefully choose to do so, they don't sit around and wait for "chance" or some external influence to bring them success. Nor do they expect to magically discover the solution to their problems, they work hard mentally and/or physically, to achieve their goals with a definite aim in mind. They're usually so determined to achieve something, that it doesn't matter what obstacles may come their way. The same applies to an addict who desires to become an ex-addict, you must overcome your old thinking no matter how difficult it might seem. Recovery from addictions isn't a gift you receive, rather it's your reward for persisting to dwell upon the right types of thought. In retrospect, if you persist in continually thinking about your addictions and the hold they have on you, you'll continually end up right back in them. Now before you quit reading my book because I said this would require some work, you should also know that it's not as complicated as you might suppose! Keep Reading!

Global Wretchedness?

It is a fool who believes that a
person of strong character has somehow
never had to deal with the pressures of an
addiction, or difficulties in life, for
that matter. They believe perhaps that the
successful were either born with a silver
spoon in their mouth, or just raised into a
"good" family. On the contrary, strong
character is formed by the discovery of a
particular weakness in your character and
willfully choosing to rectify it.

It's also quite foolish for someone to
view or perceive a persons success as
merely the result of luck or chance and
that anyone whose ever become rich or
successful, must have either swindled or
cheated their way to the top. The fool is
also likely convinced that wretchedness is
the state of all humanity. After all, if
they themselves are unable find success or
dig out of the misery they're surrounded
by, how then has anyone else been able to
truly do so either? Many people believe
that the rich and successful are either all
liars or in some fashion are just
dishonest. Why do I believe they have this

narrow minded view of the world? Well it's quite hard to swallow, but I've been both the fool and an addict for the better part of my life and after finally moving to the other side of that, I can admit to it. I'm not rich at this point by the way, I wasn't trying to make that claim.

Addiction is weakness

Addiction on any level is without a doubt the result of a weakness in character. Smoking, drug abuse, addiction to pornography, gaming, gambling, hoarding, overeating, and much more are all the result of this weakness, at least when you break them down. Maybe you've already grasp that fact and so have advanced even further toward your goal of overcoming addiction! I congratulate you once again! Understand right here and now though, the mere possession of knowledge isn't enough to create true change for you! It's only through the application of knowledge that you can hope to achieve and accomplish your goals. If you're unable to come to grips with that, you'll always remain a slave to whatever has mastered you.

Chapter 3

Chapter 3   My View of Addiction

The 3 levels of addiction

I've classified addiction into three basic levels in order that I might discuss the varying types of treatment an addict may require. I believe that all but the first level of addiction requires the same treatment, which I also refer to as the "severe level". This would be the point at which a behavioral addiction or substance dependency is so completely out of control, that it will have nearly consumed your entire ability to reason. It's also quite possible at this level that the addict could likely careless whether they live or not, as long as they had a drug in their system. It's due to this unstable state of mind, that they'll likely need immediate medical care and if necessary, to begin the process of detoxification. I do realize, that while under the influence of such a overpowering substance, it's highly unlikely they'd even be reading this. So if you know someone at this stage, please get them to a facility where they can receive medical treatment. After they've been through detoxification, then direct them to this book.

The second level would be when there's a substance dependency or a behavioral addiction present, but the addict is still able to make somewhat rational decisions. They should be able to realize if they don't soon change directions, their pursuits will likely begin to cause tremendous loss. Not to mention suffering the consequences of criminal punishment. If that indeed did happened, they could also lose their liberties as a normal citizen and most likely their career, family (if they had one), as well as to permanently destroying their reputation.

Then there's the last level, which I use to categorize people who all but deny the fact that they even have a problem. As their issues may seem so insignificant they likely won't even recognize a need to change. Believe it or not, it's the people in this third stage which are actually the hardest to help, but still not impossible!

It's not a problem.

Let me begin by discussing those who are in the third level. These individuals oftentimes see their "small issue" as merely a distraction, or perhaps a way to soothe themselves while they're trying to get through a tough time. They likely won't view their vice as an addiction, because they sincerely believe it just helps them to cope. This "help" can be labeled anyway you want, but you likely have an addiction nonetheless. There's an attitude which goes along with this denial that bothers me horrifically. Mainly because it's the same one I've personally adopted several times throughout my own life. It's the attitude that "life's too short so you should just do whatever feels good"! However, I think my all time favorite line has to be, "you gotta' die from something"! If you believe that having fun is found in the abuse of a harmful substance or in the act of indulging yourself, I'm afraid your definition of fun is grossly misunderstood. Please understand I'm not pointing fingers at anyone, as I'm not some guy whose been a "saint" his whole life. Truth is, 15-25 years ago, I was a true hell raiser with the best of them. I deserved on many days to have been thrown in jail, or killed as a result of the

ignorant and destructive things I did.
Maybe I was just "smart", or "lucky", and
that's how I've escaped death and the
consequences of the law as many times as I
did. You should know too, that I'm not at
all proud of my past, because there were
many times I'd boast to anyone who'd listen
to me, about how I could out run the cops,
or how I did things to people or their
property and got away scott free. Maybe I
did "get away" in some way, but the after
effects of that lifestyle took its toll on
me as I got older. I paid for my foolish
actions by the losses I suffered as a
result of being that type of person and I
now perceive that lifestyle as someone who
has no respect for themselves, or those
around them. To me, this is the true
definition of a pagan! Anyway, at one time
I may have strongly disagreed with being
labeled something so extreme and my family
(for the most part) believed I was a decent
young man. Unfortunately my actions proved
otherwise and I'm able to admit to this now
because I understand that happiness is the
result of being of good character, not
through careless and reckless indulgence!
Being a pagan leads you into a life of
slavery, as actual freedom is defined by
the ability to make choices for yourself

and not through permitting a debilitating drug or destructive behavioral pattern to make them for you.

Addictions have devastating effects.

Have you ever watched someone suffer the effects of the disease called emphysema? I've personally watched someone dear to me suffer and it wasn't easy to watch, I assure you. To see the pain and disappointment on their face simply because they were unable to physically do anything for themselves, is to say the least quite depressing. It's with no less then pure sympathy for all the victims of this disease, that I must reiterate that a persons life is only worse as a result of them having been a smoker! What's crazy, is this person I was close to had only smoked as a young man, but yet he still suffered greatly because of it. Let's not forget to mention the other zillion issues you can develop as a smoker, and how literally every single year millions and millions of people loose their loved ones to ignorance and stupidity. I apologize once again if I made anyone feel bad by calling them dumb, I just call it like I see it. It's not just the "smokers" who are dumb, I've been an idiot myself! I smoked and chewed tobacco for well over half of my life and now I just pray my family won't have to suffer because of my past selfish choices!

"I feel sorry for some people"

Not only have I read countless stories of people who've fallen victim to drug abuse, I've personally witnessed the lives of several friends who went broke and lost everything because of crack cocaine and meth. They lost their jobs, possessions, reputations, friends, and self-esteem in exactly the same way I did. This doesn't include the countless stories I've been told by random strangers about their addictions or how some addiction ruined the life of someone that they know.

I'd like to tell you about some of the encounters I've had over the years and how I have seen first hand the living conditions that drug abusers can often find themselves in. There was such an instance when a friend of mine and I were viewing various properties available for sale in a lower income area (for investment purposes). This one particular abandoned home I'll never forget as long as I live. It turned out this property was being used by the local "druggies" as a "crack house" and in case you've never been in one, you can't imagine the animalistic conditions addicts will tolerate in order to abuse drugs. You can probably guess without me painting a Picasso, that if there's no running water, no working sewage system, and 10-20 people sharing a small space, that the conditions are going to be "slightly" unsanitary. Let's just put it this way, I could smell the stench permeating out of this house before I got within 10 feet of the front door! Regardless of the stench, we ignorantly walked in anyway and gagged immediately upon entering. As we hesitantly walked around, we discovered that there were used hypodermic needles, burnt soda cans and used prophylactics everywhere and the dirt was at least an half inch thick on the floors. The walls were riddled with holes and there where multiple places where people had fallen through the ceiling. Anyway, it became so bad, even after I held my shirt over my mouth and nose, I still ended up gagging before going back outside. Honestly we shouldn't have even been in there without some sort of proper protective gear, but we were quite curious and a little dumb at the same time. Needless to say, for more than obvious reasons we didn't buy the property. What a horrible mess and such a tragic thing to imagine where you'd have to be mentally to endure these conditions.

There was another time when I had this job where I was responsible for repossessing furniture and big screen T.V's. It wouldn't have been quite so bad, except I was required to go into homes in some rather poor areas of town (ghetto type areas). I discovered rather quickly that many of these customers who were renting from our company, were often raising their families and children in utter filth. On one occasion I went into this home where there were literally pathways of dirty clothes mixed with garbage, lining the floors of their entire home. I was there to repo a 60" Wide Screen Projection TV out of this one persons very tiny bedroom. On one of the walls in this room was a single bed, it was covered with used baby diapers, a half empty pint of liquor, empty beer cans, trash, cigarette butts and crumbs of food. The TV I was taking out was a foot away from the bed and all I could think about was the $200 a month payment they were making at one time on this thing and how their priorities in life couldn't have been further off. Don't get me wrong I'm sure there are worse stories out there, I wouldn't doubt it for a moment. Those these experiences were an eye opener for me, at this point in my life, I still couldn't see any correlation between the consequences of being a drug abuser and what was soon to be my future.

I'm truly not trying to "out do" any stories here that others may have concerning the toll that drugs and alcohol can have on a persons life. However, I'd still like to share one last story as this is perhaps the saddest story I've ever been told, at least from a first person perspective. This young boy around the age of 9 or 10 years old, who I ran into during a visit to a local public park, was walking and bouncing his basketball as our paths crossed. I noticed he was all alone and then he looked up at me, so I smiled at him and asked if he was lost? He said nope, so then I asked if his mom and dad knew where he was? (as he seemed a little young to be all alone in such a big park) He began to explain in very polite tone that his dad was in prison and his mother was killed

when he was younger. He told me he was
living with his aunt or someone like that
and they lived right down the street. I
said ok and was about to walk away from
him, but he began talking to me again. He
proceeded to describe to me in detail how
his mom had died. He told me he was in his
bedroom playing and his dad was outside
grilling in the backyard. His mom had
fallen asleep on the couch in the living
room, when all of a sudden his dad came
into the house yelling and screaming at
her. So he dropped whatever he was playing
with and rushed into the room to see what
was going on. That's when he walked in and
discovered his dad standing over his mother
with the grill held high above his head. He
continued yelling and cussing at her, when
suddenly his dad threw the open grill at
his mother, knocking her out. The red hot
coals from the grill went everywhere and it
wasn't long before the couch was on fire,
and then the entire house. I assumed his
mother must have been killed instantly, or
had died at some point due to the severe
burns she must have suffered. However, he
didn't finish telling the story, because he
heard someone calling his name and had to
leave. Honestly, I felt as though I'd just
sat and watched a two hour horror film or

something, but what's crazy about his story was the fact that he literally had no emotion as he told it. Not one single tear, and no facial expressions, he calmly told it as if he were telling me a story about how tall the grass in his backyard can get or something. I can't begin to imagine what his life must have been like up that point to be emotionless recalling such a horrific story like that. Maybe he was in denial that it had really happened, or perhaps he'd told the story to so many people, that he'd simply become numb to it. Anyway as I said, that's probably just one of the millions of stories about people who suffer as a result of drugs or alcohol.

What's wrong with people?

Have you ever observed the behavior of someone in the final destructive stages of a drug like crystal meth? Well I'm pretty sure that's what I had observed one afternoon as I got behind this lady driving her car down the highway. As I came up beside her, I noticed immediately her hair was a tangled mess and her face was all covered with deep pitted scars. She looked as though she was pretty out of it and was steadily banging her fist against her head like there was no tomorrow. I don't mean banging like she'd forgot to have her V8 that morning either, she was hitting herself so hard and so many times in a row, I literally thought she was going to knock herself out. I considered reporting her to the police from my cell phone and probably should have, simply for the safety of those around her, but for some reason I just didn't. Seriously it's very sad and tragic to imagine how miserable a persons life must be in order for them to partake in such mind altering drugs. Like I've said, I've never had an addiction to crack or meth so I cant relate to the feelings associated with crashing after using them. I can however relate to being so bad off that I regularly risked my life and reputation to indulge myself in my addictions. Then there was also the consequences of my addictions which cost me my marriage, my home, my cars, full-time custody of my child and not to mention every ounce of hope that I'd ever be anything other than an frigging addict.

I'm not affecting anyone else

As deluded as an addict can become, they often think the consequences of their addiction only affect themselves. That somehow our families and those we care about, somehow go unaffected by our decisions. We ignorantly believe we're able to do whatever we want, because no one else will have to suffer for our choices! We tell ourselves that anyway, because deep inside we know we're affecting other people by our decisions, but we ignore it so we can get our fix. That's why anything of an addictive nature is simply the pursuit of the selfish, because if you really cared about yourself, or your family, you wouldn't put them in a position of loss just to satisfy yourself.

Casting the blame

It's probably no big secret that addicts possess an innate ability to use people, situations and events to their advantage. What types of situations do you suppose could best give an addict excuses for not having to maintain self-control? How about being able to blame a medically

diagnosed condition or disease on their
addiction? Then they could blame their
"condition" on what's causing them to
partake in their habit. What a relief that
would be, right? I guess it would then be
possible too, for a mental illness to
compel someone to indulge themselves in the
pleasures of their flesh. Like perhaps
choosing to go on a drug or alcohol binge
and having illicit sex with multiple
partners? I mean after all, if there's a
disorder causing their problems, couldn't
they just do whatever they wanted and get
away with it? Come on, really? What fool
created that crap? The unarguable fact is
that we become uncontrolled when we give
our control over to something. There are no
real mental illnesses that are able to
force us to do things we don't first will
ourselves to do. The people or person(s)
who created these types of excuses or who
support them, do so to justify their own
lack of self-control. The religious often
do the same thing, but they blame "demons"
for the reasons they're unable to control
their actions. Don't be fooled by any of
these "blame shifters" and fall for their
religious or medical explanations as to why
a person lacks the ability to control
themselves. These things are just lies and

excuses fabricated by zealots who likely just want to boast about how they've unlocked the mysteries and perplexities of addiction. There are no mysteries, the cause isn't perplexing, there's no reason other than our choosing to create "pleasure or pain" for ourselves. Allow me to explain this a bit further. The only variation between a person who can't help themselves and a person who can, is the ability to willfully choose which things they'll allow themselves to be involved with. Choice is never removed from us as the result of a demonic possession or a faux mental disorder, even as "sound" as some of the explanations may seem. These excuses were conceived purely as an attempt to remove or reduce accountability. I'm no "expert" though and since I'm not a Ph.D and don't possess a doctorate or even a college degree for that matter, I couldn't possibly be capable of explicating the complexities of human mental illnesses. I suppose too, that I'd be incapable of comprehending the psychological imbalances induced by synthetic chemicals infusing with those naturally produced by our brain? You're probably right because after all, really all I am, is an ordinary guy who was once an addict to multiple vices and now I'm not.

Sorry for venting, let's get back on topic. An addict also often views others in society as being free to indulge themselves whenever they please, so the question they ask themselves is why shouldn't I? This further adds to their "bank of excuses" and reasons to do as they please. The ugly truth, is that the majority of the people they observe who appear to be having "all the fun", realistically aren't having that much fun! At least not the ones who are all "doped up" on drugs. They're actually falsely advertising a life of someone who's truly happy. This "happiness" they've convinced themselves they're having, is nothing more than a temporary mindset, as their altered state of bliss will turn quickly into disappointment and frustration. This happens to anyone who abuses drugs or alcohol or indulges in the acts of luxuria. The discontent created by their temporary mood explains the addicts perpetual need to constantly re-create their false happiness, and thus defines the stronghold of addiction.

Who and what did I blame?

I personally placed a lot of my
blame for my addictions on my parent's,
because they didn't effectively teach me
about sex, drugs and alcohol. Honestly
though I think they just didn't know how to
approach the subject (as is the case of
most parents). I also cast a lot of blame
on my wife for not "pleasing me" enough,
thus the reason I blamed her for why I
ended up in a lot of the mess I found
myself in. Which in the end, in some
fashion, contributed to the demise of our
marriage. So then, why is it that an addict
feels the need to cast the blame of their
addiction on someone else? Simply put, it's
just easier that way! After all, it
dismisses us from having to look at
ourselves for the reason's we fail. It's
also much easier to justify ourselves when
we don't have to take personal
responsibility for our actions! I've
discovered one of the main reasons addicts
project the responsibility of recovery on
those who care about them, is because when
the treatment or recovery program fails to

work, they have instant excuse to blame someone else for it not working!

It's my little secret.

I believe that the majority of addictions are performed in secrecy, unless it's something which is seen as socially acceptable. Really though, I think it's just because we don't want our peers or loved ones judging us for what we do. At least judging is what we accuse them of doing, even if all they may have is concern that we maybe doing something harmful to ourselves. In our scheming and secrecy all we're actually doing is devolving as a species. It's easy for us to become like rodents hiding in the shadows and scattering about in order to perform our selfish acts in privacy. We foolishly believe too, that while we're in the secret places that we hide, that somehow there will be no consequences to our actions. That they'll be mystically hidden from others in the distance of space and time. We only fool ourselves though, because there are always deeper consequences than merely being caught in the act. Especially since some addicts may never be caught!

What happens, is ultimately our addictions take something out of us, they zap our energy and rob us of our confidence. They prevent us from giving to others, the way that we should and like I've said before, the only thing selfishness leaves in it's wake is self.

Before I move on to another subject, I want to discuss for a moment what I refer to as the "ugly step child of secrecy". Which are the acts of the exhibitionist, as they prefer to indulge themselves in their addiction while in the presence of others. It seems to give them a more intense rush to expose their guilty pleasures to the world. How do I know all this? I've had addictions through out my twenty-five years as an addict where I did some of these same things and know first hand the bondage they create.

I'm not here to harp.

Truly I can't convey enough, my purpose with this book isn't to harp on anyone! Instead I can most definitely sympathize with the types of situations people often find themselves in. Especially with the way we've all been taught to deal with our addictions, which is pretty much not at all. Besides, pestering someone about what they're doing wrong, only drives them further away. When you continually bug someone about what they do they'll simply begin to hide their addictions from you. If you persist, then they'll eventually try to detach themselves from you so they can do what they want. It's also possible for the person who's trying to help, to become seen as nothing more that a "nag" and then you'll eventually become despised and they'll likely avoid you at all cost. The bottom line is that, pestering is unproductive, if not detrimental to the addicts recovery!

Escape reality?

The main reason a person seeks solace in the temporary delusions provided by their addiction, is their desire to escape reality. They then begin to recognize that their situation is progressively getting worse, but yet they ignorantly return to the very thing which put them there in the first place! This whole process mimics insanity and perfectly illustrates why nothing of an addictive nature truly ever produces the "effect" we were originally hoping for. In fact, it does the opposite. Instead of freedom, it puts us in a position of slavery and as I've found out the hard way, freedom and true happiness are only obtained through the exercise of self-control. As you'll learn to be self-controlled, you'll be able to choose the quality of your life and not leave it in the hands of your addiction.

Chapter 4

Chapter 4   Just the Tip

I went to a counselor, once

    I'd like to tell you about the first and only experience I've ever had with an addictions counselor. I must admit, I was quite apprehensive to go to one in the first place, as I wasn't sure it would really do me any good. I'm more than certain this was due to the fact I'd fallen victim to my pride, as I thought I'd already figured everything out on my own and so didn't need someone else telling me how to change. I did decided to give it a shot anyway, mainly because I was urged by a friend to go. Despite my pride, it did seem as though my addictions were beginning to get more and more out of hand! So I drove 2 hours to meet with this person, which was a little rediculous, but I figured he must be really worth it. Anyway, after some initial chit-chat, he noticed my attention quickly shift to a painting hanging on his wall, which was of an iceberg of all things. He asked me if I'd realized that the the tip of it was the only visible part sticking up out of the ocean, that the bottom part was typically hidden beneath the surface of the water and was in fact much larger in proportion to the exposed top. I just so happened to be aware of that fact, as I'd previously seen various television programs explaining what pierced the hull of the Titanic and eventually caused it to sink. He proceeded to explain how my specific problems were a figurative iceberg and my addictions were just the surface of what was a much larger problem underneath. It wasn't until many years later though, that I'd discovered just how true this fact really was. However, I now also realize that as an addict, an awareness of this magnitude was actually quite counterproductive to my recovery. Mainly because this analogy made me uncomfortably aware that my recovery was going to be long and drawn out. If you know anything about addicts, most of us don't want to have to wait for something, we want it all and we want it now! Anyway, it also became quite evident this was going to be a very expensive venture and I began to convince myself that he was simply after my money! Then sure enough, when our hour was up, he tried to set up an appointment for us to get together again! All I could envision was his hand reaching down deeper into my wallet! Before you judge my analysis of the situation, I'm sure he truly wanted to help me, so I'm not going to get preoccupied with attempting to reveal his true intent. However like I said, as an addict I perceived the whole session as an intricate plan to enlarge my problems, necessitating what was sure to be an entire series of expensive sessions. As far as intentions go in a situation such as this, I don't believe they amount to a hill of beans. It's more about what perception is formed in the mind of the intended subject. I must admit, there's a certain cleverness behind the whole iceberg analogy. However, in the end, this whole situation was simply another brick in my wall. A wall which was blocking my road to true freedom.

Some issues with traditional recovery

I've discovered through personal experience that an addict generally governs their affairs by the feelings or emotions they have at any given time. That when there's any change in their emotional state, their desire to indulge themselves becomes the strongest. So whether or not they're going from being happy or sad, or

excited to disappointed, as a result of
this rise or fall they'll experience a
change in the chemicals naturally released
in their brain. It's often this unwelcome
change that triggers their need to
counteract those natural chemicals. It
happens all the time and is the "chemical
explanation" as to why addicts choose to
abuse.

What's unfortunate about these natural
chemicals and how they're released into our
body, it's that they never cease to present
themselves, not even during the attendance
of recovery meetings. Therefore it's
important, especially during these times,
to be aware of the triggers which often set
an addict spiraling in the wrong direction.
Some of these triggers have managed to
incorporate themselves into many of the
traditional recovery programs. In case
you're wondering, I've participated in some
of them, or at least some version of them.
I mainly attended them to support a friend
of mine who had some severe drug
addictions. This friend was also my co-
worker and was living in a half-way house
with a dozen or so other drug addicts. Two
to three times a week, I'd drive 45 minutes
out into the middle of nowhere to pick him
up to try to get him some different types

of help. At the time, I think the only help he was getting was what was required in order for him to live at the half-way house. The reason I bring all this up, is I'd like to discuss in a little more detail, what I feel are the implications of bringing a group of addicts together for the purposes of recovery. I believe a lot of these meetings, including the ones I attended, were designed to encourage addicts to "open up" and share their concerns or issues about how their recovery was going. Also, to do other things such as confess how long it'd been since they last used, and also to share any success stories they may have had. It's not difficult to see how it could be beneficial for addicts to share success stories with each other, but where the problem occurs is when the addict begins to explain how and why they "messed up". These admissions can be quite harmful to the other addicts in the group, as I will further explain. It was often at the end of these meetings, that I'd walk away with overwhelming feelings of hopelessness. Number one, that I'd ever be anything other than a recovering addict, and instead of discovering anything useful to help me with my own addictions, I'd discovered some new and innovative ways to indulge myself in my own pleasures! Which is crazy I know, to suggest that a time tested and widely accepted recovery program could possibly be counterproductive to an addicts recovery. However, as I've learned in life, sometimes you just have to call it like it is. In this case, if it walks like a duck and talks like a duck, it must be a duck! It's quite important then, for an addict to grasp the fact that whether or not they'll admit it, they're always "tuned in" to discovering new and inventive ways to indulge in themselves (even if it's during a recovery meeting).

This reminds me of a few stories I've heard pertaining to some recovery programs based around sexual addiction. They have similar style meetings to what the drug abusers have, but they're specifically designed for people addicted to sex. Anyway, there were often members of these groups that would end up having sex with each other after the meetings. No surprise there right? Well, they'd confess later that the reason they did, was because they were aroused by their co-members explicit confessions. Did you feel anything just then when you read that? Those are the chemicals I am talking about which can trigger countless numbers of things. If you didn't feel anything, it's perfectly fine, it just would've made a good example of what I mentioned earlier.

I have some news for those of you who've never actually been an addict and who perhaps don't fully understand the logical, or more likely "illogical", thinking we can have. These paticular thoughts, are more often than not, geared toward making up whatever excuses that are necessary in order for us to abandon our recovery efforts. If I could ever come up with just one good reason as to why my recovery efforts weren't working for me, it would give me the perfect excuse to do whatever I wanted.

Moving on, I do comprehend the principles behind bringing people together into a group, however I can assure you with nothing less than with my total conviction, that it's truly the last thing you want to do for the sake of an addicts recovery. Giving addicts the opportunity to relate with each others struggles, simply deepens their camaraderie and further fuels their excuses to do what they want!

Who came up with the group idea?

Where then did this idea of grouping addicts together come from? My theory is that it was during a time when perhaps "the experts" began to consider addicts as outcast members of society. So they decided to alienate them by putting them all together in groups, the same way that criminals are. If we're all being honest, isn't that really how most of us perceive addicts anyway? That for the most part, they're all just shy of being criminals? It could be that they're already criminals and therefore they deserve to be put with their own type? Do you think it's really possible that people think that way? That addiction somehow only captures the will of a few select group of derelicts? I find rather than it being an isolated issue involving only a few members of society, that it's truly more of an epidemic, affecting the multitudes. At least that's what I gather from the conversations I have with random everyday people that I run into.

I think it's time to restructure

There are likely a number of success
stories stemming from these traditional A&R
programs and most of the intentions of
these programs seem to be honorable.
However, that doesn't mean they're creating
freedom for these addicts! It's entirely
possibly that they're being taught nothing
more than a different form of slavery.
It's due to this realization that I'm
amazed, despite the level of advancement
we've been able to achieved in the last 100
years, that these types of outdated
programs still exist. I suppose it could
be due to the fact that no one's come up
with a better or more effective
alternative? Maybe any alternate recovery
programs which have become available, have
been shot down by the mainstream community
of so-called experts? Nonetheless, I
believe as experts or ex-addicts we can all
agree with one thing. That we tend to
become like those we're around the most! So
then why would you surround struggling
addicts with other struggling addicts?
Doesn't make a whole lot of sense when you
think about it, does it? It would be like
putting a group of a dozen or so non-
swimmers together in deep water without
life preservers and then having a life
guard yell out to them instructions on how

to swim. Do you get my point? When a person is drowning and you're within a few seconds of suffocation, you'd deliberately drown your own mother if she was all that was there to grab onto. The same applies to the addict, they'll always prefer to drag someone else with them when they're going down, so they won't feel quite so alone. Alright, so there's no more hiding my true feelings. It's probably more than obvious at this point that I'm not a fan of some of the practices of the traditional recovery programs. It's not even that, I just want people to at least have a fighting chance at overcome their addictions!

What does an addict need?

So then, what does an addict need? Everyone's likely heard the old saying, "that bad company corrupts good character, right? Well, is bad company limited to corrupting those of good character? I think not. If I was given the opportunity to re-word that saying, I'd change it to, "bad character is best rectified in the presence of good company" and that's exactly where I'm coming from with this book. It's my conviction, at least in terms of recovery, that the only relations an addict should have are with a person who truly understands the points that I make in this book. If you insist on having meetings to help addicts recover, begin with teaching them how they can develop self-control and how they are able develop their character with the *proper wisdom*. Don't try to convince them that they're powerless and must be controlled like a robot in order to overcome their addiction!

Look, I realize there are good intentions behind many of these programs. They seem to be based around giving your life over to God and I do agree 100% with that idea, because if you don't believe in a higher power you're literally on your own in terms of your recovery. Any wisdom truly able to set a man free from his vices, originated from God in the first place. Unfortunately many of the existing programs are designed to keep addicts within an arms reach of relapse. Why, because at every step they're reminded of their addiction and their inability to make choices. Which in turn keeps them bound to slavery, even more so as they become more and more convinced they're powerless to overcome their addiction. The problem is that you should never allow anything or

anyone to take control of your will, not
even God. Now before you accuse me of
being a heretic, I want you to switch the
words from "God direct my will", to "God
steer my ship for me" and I will hopefully
be able to explain what I mean. Truth be
told, God's desire has always been to
"guide us" not "control us". He wants us to
use the wisdom he supplies in order to
learn how to steer our ship. Unfortunately
there are many religious zealot's who
believe that God should be the one that
steers, that he should indeed be in "direct
control" of our will. My response to that
would be, if it were truly God's desire to
control us, what then is the purpose of the
"light"? Be honest, do you really believe
it's God's place to do everything for us,
to guide our lives as well as to control
our will? Wouldn't that simply make us
robot's? If you're still having trouble
with this idea, then I'll plainly spell it
out for you, why it's not God's desire to
control our will. It's for the exact same
reason that hatred must exist in the world,
which is to provide a contrast to love,
because without this contrast there's
nothing by which a comparison can be made.
Without being able to maintain control over
our will, we wouldn't be able to prove our

devotion to anyone specific, or to do make any decisions in life for that matter. Think about it, without light there'd only be darkness, without the capability of feeling sorrow, you'd only be capable of experiencing happiness. Then your emotional state would always remain the same and the result would most certainly be insanity. You wouldn't even be able to morn the loss of a loved one, because your emotional state would never change. You wouldn't be able to choose just one person to marry, because you'd love everyone the exact same way. Without contrast, everything in life would be mundane. God knows what he's doing and it's because of his perfect design of "free will" that we must learn to control ourselves and not depend on him to do it for us. God's in the business of guiding, not controlling. He created laws for us to follow, so we'd have a guide and that's it. When men became legalistic about those laws it took away they're intended purpose. Anyway, this isn't a theological debate, bottom line is that without free will it would have been completely useless for him to create any laws in the first place. Without the freedom to choose between what's right and what's wrong, we would truly become robotic and incapable of human emotion. Sorry to keep dragging this subject on and on, but it would be the same as trying to teach a computer how to love, when it's completely incapable of doing so. Why is it impossible? Despite the fact you'd be able to program it with varying commands and responses, it could only choose from those defined set of commands. Yes you could give it parameters and boundaries, then it would be able to compare those things with the laws you previously gave it. At some point, it's true, it could make suggestions or answer your questions. However, it will never be capable of choosing anything irrational, nor can it deviate from the specific pre-programmed instructions you previously entered into it. It's the same with human beings, without being able to deviate from the commands given to us, we would be incapable of free will.

Chapter 5

Chapter 5   My mess and how I overcame it

The first addiction I ever developed, was when I was a kid to playing video games and I remember clearly what started it all. It was a video game called Donkey Kong and it was to a game system I got for Christmas one year called Colecovision. I think I received it as a gift from Santa and even though it started out only as a few hours here and there, it ended up being an obsession for me. When I was home during summer vacations, there were days I literally didn't even make it outside because I couldn't stop playing! I know that hardly seems like something that would merit being labeled an addiction, as I'm sure there are likely many children exposed to far worse things. Nonetheless, it's where it all started for me. Regrettably this obsession didn't end at childhood, in my adult years I became so obsessed with computer games, I'd stay up until 4 to 5 a.m. as my wife slept alone in our bed. I can't totally blame this as the entire reason why my marriage fell apart, but I certainly missed out on a lot of "marital activities" that would have been taking place in lieu of the stupid computer games.

Anyway back to when I was a kid. It wasn't long after the video games became an obsession, that a friend of mine and I figured out you could watch certain scrambled cable channels after midnight and see some "pretty interesting" things. I also clearly remember some very vivid and memorable feelings associated with the first time I ever observed a clothes-less female in person (not my mother of course). I have memories too of the first time I ever took a drag off a cigarette as a pre-teen and the first time I ever became inebriated around the age of fourteen or so. I can recall when I discovered that the internet was useful to me for more than composing and checking emails, and that's when I was introduced to a whole new set of addictions. There's a slew of others as well, but what's difficult to recall is when I actually surrendered my will over to those things, and when I allowed them to have dominion over my decisions.

I was a slave

Over the years I've indeed been a slave to many different vices, not to mention the fact I could have died from more than one of them on more than one occasion. After my repeated failures to become a man of self-control, all I wanted to do was bury my shame. The best way I found to do that was through my indulgences. There were so many times that I felt as though my addictions were somehow "there for me", when no one else was. They made me feel better, at least until the the euphoric feelings wore off. Then reality was right there waiting to slap me in the face. Each time I gave in, I immediately found relief, at least for a moment and what a fleeting moment it was! Like how fresh baked cookies smell so good as they're baking and when they're done, you grab some milk and eat a few. Only for them to come out later on the other end with a completely different aroma. That's a little gross, but seriously don't most of us start out dreaming life would be filled with endless possibility and beauty? At least until the bills began pilling up, then we just took whatever job became available. Only to spend our lives in a job that we really don't enjoy, but had to do anyway? Well maybe you can't relate to that, but that's how life was for me and the only way for me to cover that pain was with my addictions.

I accepted the blame

Twenty five years after I quit blaming everything and everyone else for my addictions, it finally became crystal clear how they'd gained control over me in the first place. I was astonished to discover that nothing had really ever been "taken away from me". Any of my decisions I made to partake in a substance or physical act, were only ever mine to make. It's imperative for you to realize and admit this too, at least if you desire to be freed from your addictions. You see, it's not until we take full responsibility for our decisions that we can sincerely hope to begin to regain control of ourselves! It only hinders our recovery when we place blame on other people, or powerless external objects for the reasons why or how we became addicted. Before I move on let me give you one more example of how I often shifted the blame. I did so by enlarging the problems of everyone else around me, as then my problem seemed rather insignificant in comparison to everyone else. I thought by doing that, somehow my consequences would be lessened as well. Anyway consequences seemed to be the least of my concerns, because once I decided to do something there was little that was going to stop me.

So we see that it's neither the circumstances, nor the temptations, which made us unwillingly to submit to our addictions! They truly never had any power over us! The only "power" that existed was the lure of enticement, because nothing in all the universe has the ability to force us to make decisions! It's always up to us to choose our vices and then we must agree with what they'll do for us before we choose to give into them. What you might be unaware of though, is that by agreeing with our vices, we're actually temporarily surrendering our will over to them. However our ability to ultimately decide what we'll choose to do, is never removed from us. The decision never gets passed on to someone or something else.

God won't control you

God doesn't want to dominate our will, so why even waste your time pleading for him to do something he won't do? Personally, I can't remember the countless times I've pleaded for him to take my addictions from me. I'd even go so far as to pray for him to remove my option to choose. However, it isn't God's place to do that, unless that is we want him to change us into robots! Even then, he wouldn't do it! It's true, you maybe powerless over what a substance or a particular behavior is enticing you to do, but you're never powerless to take control your actions! God perfectly designed the human will to be resilient to captivity and if we'd only realize that, we'd clearly see how we're empowered with an ability to overcome any and all obstacles. Any great achievement ever documented in the history of mankind, was the result of someone who'd grasped the power of the human will. In order for them to have achieved what they set out to achieve, they would've been required to first master the obstacles standing in their way.

I know at first, overcoming an addiction can seem a bit overwhelming, and can appear to be an impossible task. However, I know for a fact too, that anyone's capable of achieving whatever they've set out to do, if they'd only persist until it's achieved. Any person whose ever overcome obstacles, had to do so in the same way, by perseverance and keeping their goals at the forefront of their mind!

Seared Conscience?

After repeating the same behaviors enough times I became increasingly frustrated with myself and angry that I couldn't find better solutions to overcome my issues. This was such a viscous cycle for me because no matter how many times I'd give in, the feelings afterward were always the same, lonely and depressing.

Due to the depths my addictions descended to, my conscience eventually became something which existed only in the faintest of my memories. As I fell deeper into them my feeling of hopelessness became more and more profound. I realized I was becoming perpetually worse everyday and knew something drastic needed to happen in order for me to take back my life. Through out my book you'll find multiple references to God, however it's not my intention to promote any particular "brand" of religion. This is the reason I've not really cited any religious quotes up to this point. However, I feel I must make an exception in this one particular case. I found this verse in the Holy Bible which perfectly sums up how I knew it was time to seek any means possible to overcome my addictions. For those of you who might have Bible and want to look this up, the verse is found in 1 Timothy, Chapter 4, verse 2 and it reads; "Having their conscience seared as if with a hot iron." Truly, my conscious felt seared as though someone took a burning hot cattle prod and cut open my chest with the intentions of literally incinerating my heart. This process created a scab so thick around my heart it seemed that nothing would ever be able to penetrate it. Things became so bad for me, that after partaking in my addictions, it was like second nature to resume my daily activities without feeling any guilt. To me, that was seriously bad place to be.

An addict by nature?

All through out my life, there was always something I was addicted to. If I'd quit one thing, I'd start something else and then back again to the other thing. There was a time when I was so addicted to nicotine I'd smoke, chew tobacco, wear a nicotine patch and chew nicotine gum, one right after the other and sometimes all at the same time (except to chew gum and tobacco). Ultimately I felt as though being an addict was permanently fixed into my nature. A "design flaw" if you will. Have you ever felt that way, that you're simply an addict by nature? Sadly I began to believe that lie and from the moment that I did, I had yet another excuse to indulge myself in my addictions. Truly I felt as though God designed me with an addictive personality instead with a normal one.

What was my breaking point?

It got to the point where I gave so much control over to my addictions that my daily routine became completely based around being able to indulge in them. I'd literally plan entire days around being at the right places at the right times and literally went so far that I frequently risked loosing my livelihood. It became so out of control that there was simply no center, or structure in my life. It seemed as though nothing I did would ever end up finalized. Life was a miss-mash of time recklessly speeding by and I struggled to grab on to anything that felt good or stable. Through this rootless existence though, I've discovered how our vices gain control over us. They do so by fooling us into believing that we achieve a feeling of centeredness through our participation in them. They become like a nice warm bed on a really chilly night. If I could've snuggled up with them, I would have kicked my own wife out of the bed in order to do so.

So anyway one day after I fell on my face for what felt like was the millionth time, I was struck with a paralyzing fear that I was heading down the same old road I was on once before. The one that eventually led to the demise of my marriage the first time and also to the foreclosure of our home, the repossession of our vehicles and really everything I felt I'd worked so hard to achieve. I became so frustrated with my situation and lack of self-control, I finally decided to do something completely different from anything I'd ever tried before. Up until this point I felt as though I'd tried everything under the sun to overcome my addictions, including religion. I'd read different parts of the bible a thousand times, searching for something that would hopefully shake me up enough to cause me to change. I just couldn't understand why what I was reading wasn't getting through to me. I think perhaps I needed to hear those wisdoms put in a slightly different way in order for them to really hit home for me.

I began to seek wisdom

So, I decided to stop figuring out ways to "quit" my addictions. I began reading some self-improvement books, which honestly I usually found to be quite hokey. However, after reading some of them, I was actually quite surprised to discover that they weren't as bad as I thought they'd be. They seemed to contain consistent ideals I'd remembered reading throughout the bible (which by the way I hadn't touched in around 5 years or so). I was truly amazed at what I was finding written in these books, I discovered the authors were frequently quoting scriptures straight out of the Holy Bible. I found this quite odd, as I previously believed that the types of people who wrote books like these, were more or less just pagans who only cared about getting rich! It was quite refreshing though to find some of the same common elements of wisdom that I'd previously understood written in them. Which was exactly what I'd hoped to discover in the first place! The one bit of wisdom which stuck out to me the most was that, you become whatever you predominately think about the most. What I then discovered was this internal ability which happens to be woven right into the very fabric of our beings. It teaches us that we're able to direct our thoughts wherever we want them to be and with proper understanding and application they're able to do much more than that. It's not necessary for you to "pray" to receive this ability either, truly all you must do to begin using it is to recognize that "it" exists and that's when you'll begin to understand how to use it. In case you were wondering, you can opt not to use this ability if you choose, (by default most people don't use it) but I can't imagine why anyone wouldn't use it. Especially if they could realize the potential of it and discover in the same way I did that with proper understanding you can use it to bring forth "any condition" you desire in life! That all sounds wonderful right? I must however inform you of some potentially bad news. If you really do opt not to utilize this ability to take control of yourself, then life will end up controlling it for you. Then you'll simply be limited to accept whatever random circumstances that happen to come at you.

I began to examine myself

Being armed with this wisdom I began to deeply evaluate my life and where I had allowed myself to get to. I compared what I'd learned about my addictions with the ideas I'd just learned, and how my thoughts eventually produced the outward acts of my life. It quickly became crystal clear that all I was thinking about, was my addictions, and the serious hold they had on my life. I wanted to be different, but couldn't quite figure out how to be. What else could I expect though, all I was predominantly thinking about was my junk and how mixed up I was! Turns out, I

simply chose the wrong things to dwell upon
and therefore continually reproduced the
same outcome in my life!

Upon making this discovery, I had a
feeling similar to what I think it would
feel like if I'd found some great treasure
buried in my backyard. All I did afterward,
was read more and more and evaluate myself
even further. Every day I began to
understand my addictions like never before.
After a few weeks, I began having some
major breakthroughs and finally it
happened! It seemed like out of nowhere,
that this "light" (another influence in
choosing the title of my book) went off in
my head and things began to just make total
sense. Where I'd once only seen darkness,
suddenly there was no more! I felt as
though I'd discovered how to finally have
control over my actions! Now this doesn't
mean that I'd totally forgotten about my
addictions, however they just didn't have
quite the same "influence" they'd once had
over me. I realized too, that the things
which once tempted me, actually never had
any power to "control" me. Rather they
merely possessed the ability to "influence"
me, and trust me, there's a huge difference
between control and influence. It turns
out that my "demons" were merely taunting

me, and my re-action to them ended up being
the outcome of my lack of self control
concerning which thoughts I'd choose to
dwell upon.

All of this reminds me of a movie I've
watched about twenty times, about a guy who
was found guilty of assaulting a flight
stewardess. He was arrested and had to go
to court for it, long story short, if he
wanted to avoid going to prison the judge
required that he attend a class on managing
his anger. In this particular class was a
rather extreme sports nut who frequently
lost control of his anger while watching or
listening to sporting events. Anyway, there
was a scene when he was called out by the
therapist for listening to a game during a
therapy session. He begins his explanation
for breaking the rules, by denying the fact
that he was bothered by an error made by
one of the players during this game. He
proceeded to vividly express his feelings
about how his "anger sharks" were beginning
to swim around in his head, and therefore
was announcing his intent to loose control.
He began to explosively yell at the ball
player who'd messed up, by correcting him
and yelling out repeatedly what he should
have done. It was actually very funny, but
it's exactly the type of "shifting the

blame" I'm talking about. We tend to blame everything else, including imaginary sharks, for our lack of self-control. In this situation his "anger sharks", were simply his out of control thoughts (in case you didn't pick up on that).

Before I discovered it was my thoughts that were actually to blame for my actions, I'd always have all these dumb reasons as to why I'd give into my addictions. The most common I'd use was to cast the blame on "evil spirits". I must have figured that they would sweep down out of nowhere and attacked me while I wasn't paying attention! Truth be told, I secretly knew those thoughts were there, I knew they were hiding and building up all along. I'd covet them by pretending they weren't there and therefore I protected them, so they could eventually manifest into action! I rarely took responsibility for what I did, as it was always the monsters and demons in my head forcing me to please myself. Man was I ever deluded! I did begin to think differently once I understood that all my internal "evilness" was instead really just my out of control thoughts. "Evilness" is restricted to enticement and will never cease in it's attempts to do so. It often chooses to use the beauty of the seductive temptress to lure us, however it's totally our choice to give in and pursue her. By the way, the "seductive temptress" represents the things we're addicted to, I just used a female as an example.

Monitor your thought's!

So after becoming aware of all this, I began to train myself to monitor every thought that was attempting to enter my mind. I know what your thinking, and I was too at first, that there's a whole mess of thoughts entering our minds at any given time. So honestly this wasn't easy in the beginning, but trust me, it gets easier as you go along. I learned to pick which thoughts needed to be "illuminated" or "eliminated", beginning with thoughts like, "I sure would like some ...blank... right now", or "I just want to peek real quick" , those had to go first. I became amazed at just how many of thoughts were flying out of the woodwork throughout my day. So, it's important to take this one step at a time, removing the biggest and most profound thoughts first. Then begin to recognize the ones that seem harmless, but

as you'll discover, are able to quickly
turn into the big ones!

I thought I was finished?

The last time I relapsed and gave into
an old addiction was due to one very
distinct fact, that it hadn't been truly
"defeated" there was more that I had to
learn about it. I needed to discover
exactly what it did for me and how I was
bound by it. It was from that moment on,
that I literally picked apart and dissected
every thought that lasted for more than a
moment! I asked myself as one would enter
my mind, "is this going to help me, or is
it going to hurt me"? I even learned to
kick out the thoughts which were gibberish,
as well as the ones I felt would've had no
defined purpose behind them. You might be
thinking at this point, this guy must be
insane to suggest that a person is capable
of having that kind of control? Surely
you'd have to become mechanical in order
for it to work, but I assure you, that's
not how it works. You won't become
mechanical, because you won't ever get to a
place were you'll stop having normal or
rogue thoughts entering your mind. Even now

I have thoughts of an evil nature popping into my head, tempting me to veer off course, but I've learned to immediately replace them with better ones! Get it through your head right now, that temptations will never cease to exist in your life, don't expect them to go away! If you do, you'll find disappointment at every turn, and I guarantee your life will never cease to be a roller-coaster.

Chapter 6

Chapter 6   How to find your freedom?

Before you read this chapter, please understand that truly I'm limited on how far I am able to direct you on your journey to overcoming your addictions. I can only lead you up to the door which reveals the wisdom I've been trying to help you see. You're going to have to open it up all on your own. No one else can open it for you, not your wife or husband, not your mom or dad, neither can a therapist, priest, psychologist, psychiatrist, addictions counselor nor even God himself. You must also embrace one other very profound fact, that neither wisdom or knowledge are able to forcefully or automatically apply themselves to your life. They won't manifest in your life as a result of reading a book, or having prayed a prayer. The whole process begins with the basic comprehension, that you alone possess the power to choose your path. You're solely responsible for deciding the type of lifestyle you'll lead and by doing so, you'll begin to create a new reality for yourself. This decision is most effectively achieved by gearing your thoughts to match a specific set of desired circumstances.

You must carefully pick these circumstances
with utmost certainty, and be sure they're
indeed what you want. Because as I've
mentioned already, if you don't consciously
make these decisions, by default your life
will be directed or misdirected by whatever
random influences which happen to come your
way.

Some law's can't be broken

The following is a story I've created
just for this book, I've never used it
anywhere else and hope it will effectively
illustrate the wisdom I've come to
understand. I realize it might seem a bit
cliché, but regardless, it accurately
highlights many of the points which brought
me to understand things the way I have

It's a fact that I'm no expert on
sailing, and to be honest I don't recall
ever being on a sailboat much less sailing
in one. Nonetheless, I'm pretty sure there
are only a few basic variables determining
the direction that one will go. First would
be the strength and direction of the wind
and ocean current. Then the adjustment of
the sails to harness the power of the wind,

and finally, the position of the rudder.
With proper knowledge of how to utilize
these different variables, I'd assume you'd
be able to set sail and go just about
anywhere you wanted to. It could be that
you'll experience "smooth sailing", as they
say, or perhaps you'll run into some rough
storms and possibly some dangerous rocks.
Travel at sea can be quite dangerous if
you're unprepared for the unecpected.
Anyway, do you have the basic idea, that
this sailboat idea represents your life as
a whole. So try now to envision the ship
itself as your physical body and see your
mental thoughts as the rudder. Imagine the
wind in your sails as God (if you will) and
the storms you may encounter as
temptations, and finally the rocks as your
addictions (no pun intended!). I believe
it's fairly common to encounter storms
while on the open sea, so it might be a
good idea to prepare for them, right?
Either way, hopefully you have a strategy
to avoid becoming shipwrecked if you do
indeed find yourself caught in one. I'd
assume you'd be able to sense the
approaching storms by the changes in the
winds and the intensity of the waves, but I
suppose it's possible to miss them.
Nonetheless, before you know it, you may

find yourself smack dab right in the eye of a storm. So you'd have to quickly change course if you want to avoid being shipwrecked, or even killed for that matter. Unfortunately I have some potentially bad news for those who maybe hoping that God will somehow prevent your sailboat from crashing into the rocks. He may calm the wind or waves long enough for you to steer out of the storm, but unfortunatly you'll continue moving no matter what. It's totally up to you to change your course if you want to avoid being shipwrecked. The good news is that as you become a better "sailor" you'll discover that it's best to just avoid the storms all together, so you'll have to learn to be alert at all times.

The devil made me do it.

Do you see the correlation between the laws of science and laws of the mind in this story? The laws of nature and science state that a ship at sea will go where it's steered to go. It's also true then that the laws of the mind state that wherever your thoughts are fixed, your body will surely go as well. Let me give one more example of this law before we move on. I'd assume most of you are familiar with the most basic law of physics, which is the law of gravity. It essentially states, "that what goes up, must come down". Not that there aren't variables capable of altering this law, but I'm referring to the fundamental principles of it. So comparing these principles with the laws of the mind, specifically the ones which state that your predominant thoughts are the birthplace of your outward actions, it should become evident that you can't achieve anything without having first been influenced by the thoughts held in your mind. What's great about this law, is that it eliminates some of the ignorant ideas I've already discussed a few times. Like the ones suggesting that there's an external power capable of forcing us to do things against our will. I've gone over much of this subject already, but I want to point out once again, that it's not the "demons or monsters" controlling our minds and forcing us to indulge in our sinful pleasures! If you indeed have something "controlling what your body does", other than your own mind, I suggest you find a good exorcist or something (not that I believe in all that)! In other words, if you're trying to blame your lack of self control upon something or someone else, you're simply attempting to transfer the responsibility of your own actions upon something which is unable to do so. Despite my desire to blame something else for my faults, I'll nonetheless always be responsible for my actions, I can't blame "demons", or the "devil" as many religious zealots attempt to do. Why can't I? Because of the unbreakable laws I've just mentioned proving that these forces are unable to control or alter our will. Look, I know that sometimes it feels as if someone else is making decisions for you, and the reason it feels that way, is because we start believing there's no possible way I'm doing all this crazy stuff on my own! There must be something behind me "making" me do it. I hate to break it to you though, it's you and only you! There's never been any mystical force or capricious evil in your life forcing you to do things you don't want to do! However there are, and always will be, forces tempting you to do things.

There's only one exception to these laws, but it only applies if another human being has somehow physically overpowered you. In other words, if they've somehow managed to force you to do something you didn't want to do, that would be as far as you could go to blame something else on your actions. However, even in the aftermath of such a traumatic circumstance, we would still possess the power to re-shape our destiny and chose an alternate path. Just so we're clear too, that I'm not referring to the influences of a substance upon the mind, but rather the choices we must make before we chose to put those substances into our bodies.

The challenge

My first challenge, is for you to decide whether or not you'll continue to accept the path you're currently on, or will you begin to apply the principles I reveal in this book. Even if your not sure these principles will work for you, what can you lose by trying something different, especially if you're on a roller coaster in your current recovery regiment? Before you go any further though, it's important for you to decide what kind of person you really want to be. Do you want to be a person of strong moral character? Do you want to take command of your actions and become self-controlled? Perhaps you'd rather remain a weak, immoral and groveling person, who wastes their life on foolish pursuits? This is something you must decide for yourself, because without taking this step, it'd be useless to try any of the other steps. Please be sure not to take this decision lightly either, take as much as time as you need to decide. On the same token, don't procrastinate your decision either!

It could be that you already know what kind of a person you want to be and that's why your here, to get help with how to change. If you indeed know beyond the shadow of a doubt that you want to be a person of strong character, then move on. Otherwise, I highly suggest you find a quite room with no distractions and just sit and dwell upon the outcome of the two different lives. Do this until you know with everything in you, that you earnestly want true change. Next, I want you to stop putting any effort or energy into thoughts concerning your addictions, good or bad, even the ones having to do with quitting them. Begin instead to imagine a life in which you're the one in control, where you decide what things you're going to allow to influence your decisions! Since the word addiction ultimately means to make repeated out of control decisions, you must now begin to do the opposite. You must move toward a completely different road and you can't very well see the road leading to your freedom as long as your eyes are fixed on the one you want to move off.

Regardless of what your original reasons were for reading this book, if you desire to truly change, I'd still like for you to go into a quite room with no distractions and just sit there and be still. Begin imagining in as much vivid detail as you possibly can, how different your life is going to be as a result of your decision to be free of addictions. Try to fully envision the difference in the quality of your life, see your relationships as you want them to be, see yourself in perfect health. Are you able to do this? Understand with absolute certainty, that the road to freedom exists within you, because you won't find it anywhere else. It's ultimately about altering your habits, as the bad habits were originally formed through some sort of repeated action. In order to create new habits, you'll need to begin seeing yourself with those new habits in place, before they can actually be formed.

Quit trying to quit!

To "normal" people, the concept of
quitting a habit may seem like an
elementary concept. On the other hand, it
might be a difficult idea for an addict to
grasp, especially if they've discovered it
to be a source of pleasure. Someone who's
never quite achieved a "euphoric high" the
way some addicts have, may not be able to
fully comprehend the hold certain vices can
have. So attempting to convince an addict
to simply "quit" their addiction, without
first having understood how the addiction
has it's specific a hold on them, does
nothing more then introduce them to
insanity. Why is it insane? Because it
begins a perpetual cycle of quitting and
re-starting their habit. Ask me how I
know, as I've quit and re-started my
addictions so many times, that I simply
"quit" keeping track. Yes, I'm aware of the
occasional case when someone's smoked their
entire life and then ends up quitting cold
turkey. I'd be surprised though, if they
didn't have any choice to quit. Perhaps
their doctor or specialist informed them
that either they quit, or suffer the

consequences of a disease or illness
accelerated by their bad habit.

How to "quit" smoking

Since we're on the subject of smoking,
I'll use this as the guinea pig for how
someone can overcome their addictions. The
process begins by realizing that in order
to end an addiction, it must be replaced
with something that's not addictive. In
other words, they need to trade it for a
different "habit". I realize that smoking
is often seen as a "bad habit", nonetheless
it's an addiction. (I mention that in case
you were in denial about it) Anyway, let
me clarify a bit further on how I'm using
the word habit. I define it, as a routine
which is logically created as the result of
making self-controlled decisions, and is
made permanent through repetition. For you
to really grasp this idea, it's necessary
to have already comprehended the wisdoms
I've already discussed so far in this book.
I say that if for some reason you've
skipped the other chapters and went
straight into reading this section. (which

would be useless)   Alright, so your a "believer" then right? The first thing a smoker needs to do, is make a fundamental decision to never again put any effort or thought into figuring out how they're going to "quit" smoking! That sounds absurd right?   I can assure you that it's not. They must decide, once and for all, that they're going to begin a completely new habit (like we talked about), which will consist of thinking of nothing but fresh clean air going into their lungs. They must hold a vision of having that pure air in their lungs from the moment they wake up in the morning, until the moment they go to sleep at night. (regardless of smoking or not) This process of envisioning fresh air must also become your immediate thoughts when you get the urge to "light one up". Because if you don't form the new habit of thinking fresh air, then by default you'll remain fixed in your old habit. So the big question on the smokers mind is, do I have to stop smoking right away for this to work?   Well, I won't make the suggestion that you keep smoking, but this process doesn't necessarily require you to toss your cigarettes out the window right away. Wow, really, I get to keep smoking? Don't get too excited, the end should soon come.

Let's go a little deeper into the psychology behind this idea. All through this book there are multiple references to "mental laws" and the one I'm talking about specifically states that your body begins to do whatever your mind tells it to do. This law is also known as, cause and effect, which means that for every effect found in nature there had to first be a cause for it. For example, every human being, every tree, every plant and animal in nature, began it's life cycle as some form of seed. The germinated seed from a pine tree, will never fail to produce a pine tree sapling, at least if it finds itself in the proper environment to grow (dirt, water, sun). An oak tree, will never fail to produce seeds, and the outcome will never fail to be another oak tree. Get the point? By the way, this law can't be broken! Remember, for every cause there's always an equal effect! Otherwise we'd all be sucked into a vortex somewhere in between space and time (that's a little of my humor)! So, if you consistently envision fresh air going into your lungs (the cause) the act of inhaling bad air will begin to make less and less sense to you (which is the effect). Why, because your brain is constantly sending and receiving signals to and from your body and therefore creates corresponding actions to match your thoughts. It shouldn't be too long after you begin thinking daily and hourly, thoughts of "clean air", that your brain will soon detect a conflict between what your bodily cravings are and what your "will" is instructing it to do. If indeed you've truly convinced yourself that fresh air is what you really want in your lungs, soon your "will" should regain control and your old habit looses its ability to control you! Eventually the mere sight of a cigarette, along with the physical act of lighting and inhaling it, will begin to make less and less sense. Eventually you'll actually begin to despise the habit. Don't be disappointed though if it takes some time to for this to happen. Actually the time it takes will be directly determined by your ability to hold this vision in your mind. Therefore try to fully comprehend the idea that whatever you think about on a consistent basis (cause), is what your brain tells your body to do (effect). However, if you fail to achieve something, or in this case to quit something, realize the reason you failed was because you truly never stopped thinking about the thing you wanted to quit. Honestly this whole process works with any addiction and really with any condition you desire to change in your life.

Have a mindset of gratitude!

Next, begin to be thankful for the freedom you desire to have, even before there's any evidence of visible change. This process fuels your imagination with intricate plans on how to obtain that which you are being grateful for. So if you've lost family or friends as a result of your being an addict, begin then to be thankful for the new state of your relationships. Which should begin to change as result of your new thinking. Be grateful your for your health, for your morality and pureness of thought and whatever good and upright thing your mind can wrap itself around. Your life should begin to be in harmony with your surroundings, as well as with your friends and neighbors. Your attitude should also begin to be based around the idea, that in general, people are good and want to do the right things. On the other hand, if you just want to be a pagan, then this book will be useless to you. Overall what I am trying to teach you in this book will only work if you promote "good", because in order to attract things which are good, you must dwell only upon on those things. If you constantly allow your thoughts to remain engaged in your past darkness you'll always return to that darkness! If you think evil thoughts, you will be the essence of evil. Evil has no place in the mind which is constantly thinking good thoughts and it wouldn't be until you began entertaining evil thoughts, that they'd have the opportunity to bring forth fruit in keeping with them.

Anyway, I can't express enough how important it is for you to be grateful for your progress. What's more important is to be grateful that you've made any progress at all, even if it seems insignificant! This is important, because our addictions can still remain bitter sweet even once we're freed from them. Therefore, if you give any thought to the possibility that change will be impossible for you, then you're likely going to spiral backward. So you must immediately stamp out all doubt as soon as it enters your mind. Beat this into your head if you have to, make a mantra out of it! Believing that freedom is impossible automatically makes it impossible! Sometimes all it can take is one destructive thought to bring us all the way back down. To understand this a little better, it may be helpful for you to remember how you looked at life as a child. You believed anything was possible, at least until someone spoiled that possibility by filling your head with their diluted reality. So don't spoil your new reality now, by ignorantly allowing the wrong thoughts to remain in your mind!

God has a shovel

I've already touched on a few of the ineffective ideas which have integrated themselves into the existing recovery programs, but I'd like to reiterate some of the more important parts. These ideas have been adopted from several commonly misunderstood religious teachings and they include some corrupt ideas which took me forever to figure out weren't true. Many of these ideas I'd formed on my own, but aren't that far off from what is being taught.

Anyway, I hate to be the one who crushes your hopes as mine always were, but the hard fact is that God won't zap you with sobriety. He won't eliminate temptation from your life and won't send "his spirit" to stop your thoughts from going where they shouldn't go. "Our sins" or temptations, as I'll refer to them in this scenario, have always been the result of willful choice. If you're curious about the role God plays in the process of our recovery, it's that he provides wisdom if we'll first seek it.

You should know too that it's largely ineffective to inform an addict that God loves them and that they need to change. They're likely already aware of that and have probably heard it more times then they care to count. What they need instead, is to be taught wisdom and need a opportunity to "wrestle" with what they've learn. It's the only effective way for someone to figure out how to "dig" out of the pit of filth they're in. After all, they dug the pit, they made the decision to crawl into it and if they truly desire freedom, they'll have to figure out how to crawl out! You can't and shouldn't try to "get" them out. If you believe that God is the one who digs the addict out of their mess, your wrong. Sorry to be so blunt, but truly the only thing God provides us, is a shovel to dig with (which is wisdom). Anyway, bottom line is that God can't and won't force us to use his provision, we must grab and dig for ourselves!

You can't take my crack pipe?

Perhaps one of the most destructive ideas ever introduced, at least for the purposes of promoting internal change, is the process of forcefully separating a person from their external "trappings". To relate this to addiction and the reason why I believe it's destructive, is because the act of physically removing "paraphernalia" from an addicts use merely suspends their activities to a later time. This is largely due to their corrupted state of mind and because of this state of mind, their main reoccurring thoughts will remain fixed on their addiction, regardless if they're separated from their "equipment" or not. In other words, you might successfully remove their crack pipe from their hands and physically prevent them from inhaling more crack. You might even physically remove them from the bad part of town you found them in and get them somewhere they can get showered and all "cleaned up". Maybe you'll even feed them a nice warm meal and if your really lucky, you might get them through the process of detoxification and involved in a nice cozy rehabilitation program. However, it won't be until they realize why their addiction has been controlling them, that true change will become a reality. Why, because after they return to their old routine and get comfortable and complacent and convince their accountability partners that they're "good now", they'll simply find a new crack pipe and some crack. Because I'll bet that's all they've been thinking about, even though they may want to truly be different. If that's indeed true, it's guaranteed they'll once again go days without showering or food all just end up right back where you found them in the first place!

You say you're unable to relate to someone who's addicted to the hard-core drugs? How about someone who smokes cigarettes, can you relate with that scenario? It's still the same old song and dance with the smoker! You may preach and preach at them until your blue in the face, or until their lungs turn into a solid block of tar. You might eventually persuade them to throw out their pack of cigarettes after spending all day drilling them about how bad their habit is. You might even get to the point where you knock the cigarette straight out of their mouth because you get so mad at them for not caring about themselves. However, the solution remains the same for the smoker just as it was for the crack head. They must see why they are a slave in order to find their freedom!

The deal with Pornography

Shall we keep going? Let's look at an example of some poor sap who's addicted to viewing pornography. You could do what the hard core zealots do, which is to restrict or monitor their access to the internet and add blocks and trackers to monitor what sites have been visited. You could disconnect or restrict their cable or satellite TV access and remove all questionable movies. You could do any number of extreme things to keep someone from having any immediate porn to look at! However, you can't remove every source of pornographic material from the world! You couldn't possibly keep them from drawing things to look at, so what's the point in making an effort to remove the paraphernalia from immediately around them? Don't you get that there are a zillion sources of pornographic material available to them? Not to mention the main source which is accessible at any time and just happens to be located between their ears (thus the problem). What are you going to do when they're unable to quit running the porn videos in they're mind that they've watched every day for the last how ever many months or years of their life? Are you going to suggest to them to sit and stare at pictures of Jesus on a cross all day? Are you going to call your church group to stand and pray over them? I mean come on, really? Even if you did all that and succeeded at destroying all known sources of pornography, including the ones in their head, over time the addict would simply find or make more.

Now I'm not saying once an addict realizes what he needs to about his addictions, that he should continue to arrogantly hold on to his "stash" because he's "over" his addiction. Realistically, if those things had truly finished their work in him, he simply won't have a desire

to keep his paraphernalia around anymore.
He should toss all of it in the garbage on
his own. If you have to do it for him, then
he's not in the right place and still wants
to covet those things a little longer.
Sometimes it takes having to loose
everything before some block heads figure
it out.

I'm not suggesting you'll have success
explaining the wisdom that's able to lead
an addict to their freedom, while they're
in the act of viewing of pornographic
pictures. What I am saying is that it would
be far more effective to first provide
proper wisdom to them instead of convincing
them they're powerless and incapable of
having control over what they do. Help
them instead to understand, that with the
proper mindset, they're able to choose to
be freed from their slavery, at least if
they'll understand they're slaves in the
first place. If they don't, wisdom will
eventually show them on it's own. You see,
addicts don't need to be coerced into
following some list of rules in order to be
kept from giving into their temptations.
What you're really doing by teaching
someone those corrupt ideas, is that by the
strict observation of those rules, that
they'll be able to "manage" their

addictions. I don't know about anyone else reading this, but I don't want to spend the rest of my life "managing" my addictions! I would rather annihilate them from the source, wouldn't you?

Why are you a slave?

So then, someone desiring to be free from their addiction must first undergo the process of comprehending why it has a hold on them in the first place. It won't be until they make this discovery on their own, that they'll be able to experience lasting freedom. If you're reading this an you're trying to help an addict overcome their addiction, this whole process can truly make you feel powerless. I hope you realize though by this stage in the book, that you're indeed truly powerless to "make" someone change anyway.

So my whole point in providing these examples, is that any attempt to first alter the external circumstances of an addicts life is never anything less than temporary. I'm pretty sure some of you would agree with that, but where we may find disagreement is with the actual road to recovery. As I've pointed out, strict rules and regulations for the addict are useless, but I also believe accountability is useless and group confessionals are useless. I shouldn't use the word useless, rather they're largely ineffective. At this point this may all seem quite controversial, but if you'll stay with me, I have more points to make.

Perhaps you've heard the old saying; "you can give a man a fish and feed him for a day, or you can teach him how to fish and feed him for a lifetime". Well my saying is, "you can teach a man some rules and bind them around his neck, or you could teach him how to correct his thinking and free him from a lifetime of slavery"! Laws and rules are generally only efficient for maintaining social order and upholding justice. They're more useful for keeping tabs of a players actions during a sporting event and other things like that. However, if we've learned anything over the centuries, it should be clear that rules and legalism are largely ineffective at promoting internal change!

We must break our own chains.

Imagine if you will, noticing someone you care about sitting off by themselves in the distance. As you begin walking toward them, it appears that they're sitting in what seems to be an ordinary chair. The closer you get you begin to notice they're indeed in a chair, but they're also bound by lock and chain! Your immediate gut instinct should be to locate a key, or a set of bolt cutters, and set them free right? Before you do that, let's change the scenario and imagine instead that their chains are figurative and represent the hold their addictions have on them. First off, it could be they're unaware they're bound and may not see even the chains as you proceed to point them out. On the other hand, it could be that they know full well that they're bound, but they're simply unaware the key is underneath them! However, in order for them find that key, they're going to have to discover a few things. Up to this point, all you're able to do is make them aware of the fact that they're bound and possibly explain how they're sitting on the key. They must figure out on their own, how they're going to get it and free themselves. The same applies to the addict in recovery. Until it becomes crystal clear that they're truly bound by their vice and can learn how they became that way, they won't be able to truly free themselves. Somehow it must begin to make sense to those wanting to help addicts, that it's not our place to break chains. It's not up to God to break them either, in case that's where your religious mind was going. *Don't confuse salvation with sobriety, as it maybe God's position to save the soul, but it can only be the addicts decision to become sober.* Like I've repeated over and over, once an addict recieves the wisdom that can free him, it's up to that wisdom working in him to cause him to change! We must leave them alone and let wisdom "eat at them", until they decide to change on their own! This is no doubt where I'll loose people who are deluded into believing they that somehow possess the power to alter a persons will. You could also teach them other false ideas, such as how God can wave his magic wand over them and them be able to force them to move how he wants them to move. You could instruct them other lies too, such as, wisdom is granted through our agreement that it exists, rather than through it's application. But why waste your time and spread lies? The true definition of freedom is understood by comprehending that a persons will is bound by nothing! Bottom line, it's true that you're able to put people into a box and hang some rules around their necks and possibly keep them from their evildoings, but you can't make them choose the proper thoughts!

Will this stuff really work?

If you're unsure what I've written in this book will work for you, I'll leave the pessimist with another of my short stories. If you're someone who believes you've figured out how to overcome addiction, but yet your on a roller coaster of "ups and downs". I have to wonder if perhaps you're like the wayward explorer? He set off with high hopes to travel the world and discover distant new lands and uncover great new treasures. His first problem right from the get go, was that he began his journey with limited supplies, very limited planning and some old maps he'd won at a shady hand in poker. No sooner after he began to put some distance between himself and his starting point, he carelessly misplace his maps and ran out of provisions. He was however convinced that he was the best explorer he'd ever known, so he proceed to move forward. Predictably he quickly lost his way and discovered, after deciding to turn around and head back, that he'd forgotten where it was he'd even started from. This is a perfect example of pride followed by insanity, as there are many addicts desiring to be freed from their addiction, but may not have prepared themselves for the task at hand. However, maybe it's due to their possessing useless maps to follow? Either way, if you don't have the right tools and your maps are always leading you in the wrong direction, it maybe time to get some better tools and maps?

Chapter 7

Chapter 7   Did you give in?

This section is more of a reference to use after you've begun to apply the things you've already learned. However, you could go ahead and read it if you like, I won't tell you not to. Anyway, "giving in" is the culmination of wrong thoughts attaching themselves to each other. After enough thoughts have gathered together, they'll undoubtedly spawn and manifest themselves into an outward action. This is why all thoughts which aren't going to benefit you, need to be instantly eliminated. We must remember, evil only exists as we feed it power to exist and without the proper nourishment (which is our thoughts), it only exists in contrast to good. If a thought therefore is evil in nature and our alarm (or conscience) isn't loud enough, we must train ourselves to monitor each and every thought entering our mind. It's for this reason when we find ourselves in a situation we know could end badly, we need to be sharp and on guard to the thoughts trying to settle in. You don't want to allow any bad thought to remain, as they will indeed settle in and once they're settled in, they'll likely form into action.

Eye Candy

I'd like to make you aware of the type of thoughts which are able to sneak their way into our minds and perhaps cause us to relapse. This idea was based around addictions mainly to sex or porn, but can really be applied to any type. It has to do with justifying the way that we "covet beauty", which fuels these particular types of addictions. The first justification we use for lusting over the opposite sex, is usually the lie that we just "want to to look", and there's no harm in looking, right? We tend to believe that if we look at "a promiscuous person" using quick eye movements or "shifty eyes", that we're somehow avoiding the act of coveting. We'll simply make the claim that we're "sampling" instead of actually being fully engaging in an all out "lust fest". Usually we do this type of sampling so the "eye candy" doesn't catch you looking. The fact is, that once you sample this candy, you're likely going to want to eat it! Rarely does anyone possess enough self-control to take a sample of something they've once coveted and then decide to just leave it alone. After enough thought is given to a particular addiction, its pure foolishness to believe we won't eventually give in to it. Anyway, I'm not suggesting, either as men or women, that we should cease to notice beauty. That would be un-natural and would likely lead us into an unhealthy mental state. What I am saying, is that you'll know after you've noticed someone who's pleasant to look at, whether or not you've crossed the line. It becomes evident you're coveting or "lusting" when you begin to imagine what's beyond the lines making up the overall image of a persons beauty. The difference between noticing beauty and entering the realm of lusting, becomes obvious too if there's any shift in your state of arousal as a result of your thoughts. Just so you know this whole idea of watching what you look at and why you're looking at it, isn't about being religious. It's not about the fact that lusting over your neighbors wife is wrong. Rather what it does is effectively proves the law of cause and effect. The eye candy in this case would be the cause and the

effect would be our relapsing into an old
addiction.

Light shines in dark places

If you haven't already figured it out,
"truth and wisdom" are simply alternate
words used to describe the work of the
figurative light I used in the title of
this book. I find wherever truth and wisdom
are revealed, that "light" was already
there ahead of it preparing the way. One of
the most simple yet often difficult ideas
to grasp, is that wherever light exists,
darkness is unable to. You should begin to
realize, regardless of excuses, that it was
the light you were attempting to escape
from all along. Especially if you've
allowed your thoughts to go further than
you should. If we'd only learn to expose
our evil thoughts to this light, they'd
cease to exist and therefore allow us to
remain in freedom.

I must admit, this exposure of putting
our thoughts into the light isn't always
comfortable, it requires self sacrifice in
order to expose them. Therefore is a
person is given a knowledge of the truth

and they continually apply it to their
life, they'll not fail to produce lasting
change. This is true even in the event you
fall on your face, because in your
persistence in choosing the right thoughts,
thoughts of temptation will eventually have
a more difficult time reaching the part of
our mind that forms actions. It's the same
way that submitting to an old addiction, is
the result of your allowing your bad
thoughts to exist in your mind for too
long. However, your persistence in
thinking the right thoughts, will result in
a successful recovery. Furthermore, as you
cease to give fuel to your temptations,
they'll loose the power to influence you
and the wiser you become. Truth will guide
your thoughts as you adapt the habit of
right thinking, then you'll not just become
the master of your mind, you'll become the
creator of your destiny.

The Purpose of Relapse

Even if you've been successful at
applying the wisdoms I've revealed to you
in this book and you've also succeeded in
overcoming your addictions. Sometimes,
whether we want them to or not, an old

addiction can show back up. It's typically because it hasn't "finished it's work" in you, like I mentioned before. What does that really mean though? It's simply means you haven't discovered why that addiction had it's hold on you in the first place. There's this old saying, "that a dog returns to its vomit". I think that people have some how lowered themselves to the same level as a dog, by believing lies such as, an addict always returns to his vices. In order then to become a person of self-control, it's important that you rid yourself of any past ideas you've learned about how you'll always be an "addict". What you need to do instead, is grasp the idea that you've become a person of self-control and then always consider yourself as one. Rid yourself as well, of the slavish act of keeping up with the number of days since you've last relapsed. You won't need a reminder of days or events once you fully understand the truth about overcoming addiction. You'll be empowered with wisdom and you'll begin to understand life in a way that you never did before. Your new freedom will baffle others, especially the ones who won't understand what's happened to you.

If you fall backwards, don't cry about it, just change your thoughts! Whatever you do, don't give into the lies you'll inevitably tell yourself, like if you mess up, how you're never going to be truly different. Rather look at the step backwards as necessary in order for you to fully understand the parts of your addiction that you're still giving control over to. Stop and examine yourself again and try to remember what thoughts existed before you stepped backward. Figure out why you chose not to eliminate them. If it was for no better reason than you just wanted to do what you wanted, one more time and you keep on repeating that decision, then you need to ask yourself if perhaps you choose to overcome your addictions for the wrong reasons. In other words, go back and evaluate the original reasons you decided to seek change in the first place.

Whatever you do, never forget to monitor your thoughts! If that's truly an overwhelming concept to grasp, use an idea I used when I first began this whole process. I created a sort of "watchman", or "security guard" in my mind, who I trained to be on the "look out" for certain thoughts attempting to enter it. Really it's just being on guard to the nature of the thoughts that you're entertaining through out the day. Sometimes, I'd mess up (as you can expect to do) and I'd jokingly say to myself, "I guess my watchman fell asleep". Really it wasn't all that funny, because those thoughts typically led me to fall backward.

Lastly, never forget the heights you've attained even if you take a few steps backward. Always keep moving forward, no matter how messy it gets! This is essential, because if you build upon wisdom, you can be sure that you're building on a solid foundation. So even if you do fall back, you must realize you haven't fallen back so far that you can't recover. Anyway, if you find yourself sitting in the seat of failure, re-read this book and figure out exactly which thought's you've kept around and why. Then begin once again to build up a new fortress of good thought to keep the wrong thoughts at bay. This is a never ending process, so you should never get so confident in your new found success that you allow random or uncontrollable thoughts to remain in your mind for very long.

The man who climbed

The last short story I have is about a man who made it his aim to climb a tall mountain. Being so completely determined he prepared long before he started to climb and promised himself he'd move forward no matter what he'd encounter! Even if he lost his footing and tumbled all the way back to the bottom, he remembered before hand that he'd firmly decided to never give up until he reached the top! Envision your freedom as this mountain. Pretend that the ground is your addiction and realize you can't start to climb, much less reach your destination, until you've taken your eyes off the ground! The only reason you ever need to look down is to see where you've lost your footing, never to see how far you are from where you started!

Determination is the result of repeated effort even at the onset of potential problems. It must therefore be built up, before it becomes a real strength in your character. After all, it isn't some talent that you're just born with, it requires constant use, just like your muscles require consistent exercise to be made strong.

Regardless of what stage you get to in your recovery, I can't reiterate enough times that you'll never become impervious to relapse. You'll always retain the possibility of being enticed by temptation. You'll always be capable choosing the wrong thoughts. However, you'll always also be responsible for choosing the right thoughts, if you want to reach your goal! Be careful what you look at, what you read, and what situations you allow to yourself to become involved with. You must at all times chose what thoughts you allow to come to rest on your mind and never ever, fall asleep to this idea. Without understanding and applying wisdom, you'll never rise above the status of a fool and you'll likely never truly be free of your addictions. Begin now to train yourself to choose what thoughts you'll permit to rest on your brain, because they're all that can direct where your life will go! If you believe beyond the shadow of a doubt that true change can be yours, it will be!

In closing, I need to be clear that these wisdoms I've revealed to you are not my opinion. They're not open to psychological interpretation or evaluation, these are indeed infallible laws which characterize the most basic functions of the subconscious mind. They're practical and completely applicable, if the reader would only break down the walls of doubt and eradicate the ignorances introduced through misinterpreted theories and false wisdoms.

There's an point in life when the wise become separated from the fools. This epoch conquest began as a seed that was planted the moment we began to grasp the potential of the truth. The truth then nourishes that seed until it blooms into wisdom and that's the point at which we're able to fully comprehend, that all accomplishment originates from within ourselves!